# AURA GARDEN GUIDES

## Jörn Pinske

# Orchids

Practical advice on buying and growing
indoors and outdoors

## AURA BOOKS

# Aura Garden Guides

# Orchids

Jörn Pinske

German-language edition and photographs
*Orchideen: Die schönsten Arten und Hybriden
–Auswählen, Pflegen*
© 2002 BLV Verlagsgesellschaft mbH,
Munich, Germany

English-language edition:
© 2004 Baker & Taylor (UK) Limited,
Bicester, England
Translation: Andrew Shackleton

This edition produced by :
Transedition Limited for:
Baker & Taylor (UK) Ltd, Bicester, England

Design and picture layout by:
Studio Schübel, Munich; Peter Fruth GmbH,
Munich

Editing and text layout by:
Asgard Publishing Services, Leeds

11
Printed in Dubai

ISBN 978 1903938 50 8

Photo credits:
All photos by the author except the following:
Baumjohann: 43c, Becherer: 10, 11t, 12, 14, 19,
20tr, bl, 28t, 39t, 40l, 41t, 47b, 60t, 90t;
Blauscheck: 51; Eisenbeiss: 8, 59, 66b, 68b,
69t, 75r, 87t, 89; Floricultura: 44, 60, 61, 63b,
74b, 80, 92t; *Gardener's Chronicle*: 7t;
GBA/GPL: 53; Gerlach: 58tr, bl; Hagen: 4, 36,
37l, 66t, 71t; Krieger: 17, 41b, 47t, 54, 74t;
LENI: 33; Neudorff: 43b; Ottmann (*Der
Orchideenjäger*, 1922): 7t; Redeleit: 28b, 29t,
40r, 49; Reinhard: 37r; Rysy: 77b, 81; Strauß:
2/3, 46, 68t, 69b, 71b; Weigl: 6, 18, 48, 56,
58br, 63t, 64, 67, 72b, 75l, 77t, 82, 83, 84b, 91,
92b; Zunke 43ac.

Illustrations: Heidi Janiček
Map page 13: Jörg Maier

# Contents

# The world of orchids

The Maori people of New Zealand believe that orchids are not of this world. The gods planted them in the gardens of the stars, then poured them out over the trees and mountains to announce their arrival.

## Orchids in history and legend

Orchids used to be very rare and expensive plants, and thus only available to the privileged few, while nowadays they can be bought at reasonable prices from any flower shop or garden centre. Yet they have remained just as strange and fascinating as they ever were.

The magic of orchids is due not only to their strange yet beautiful flowers, but to their weird lifestyles and methods of propagation. They are a fascinating plant family surrounded by many legends that lend them an aura of mystery and exoticism. Such legends come mainly from the writings of early plant collectors who went in search of riches and adventure.

Benedict Roezl (1824–85) collected plants in Central and South America, where he discovered other flowering plants as well as orchids, not to mention various plants of economic importance.

◄ Miltoniopsis 'Robert Strauss' – often sold as Miltonia 'Robert Strauss'. Miltonia orchids were once thought to be particularly difficult to look after, but we now know that they were simply being kept too cold. However, they do need a very humid environment.

Their stories go well beyond the simple facts, because they would exaggerate the dangers to discourage competitors, and would even give wrong information about where they had found their plants so as to prevent other collectors from 'stealing' from their patch.

Among these collectors were some with a genuine interest in botany – young European gardeners of great courage, stamina and enterprise, possessing an overwhelming interest in the plants themselves.

One of these orchid collectors was Benedict Roezl (1824–85), who began his gardening career in Bohemia at the age of only 12. His work eventually brought him to Mexico, where he ran a tree nursery, and for almost 40 years he collected orchids and other plants from all over South and Central America. He once sent back 10,000 orchids from Colombia and 3,000 *Odontoglossum* from Panama. Thanks to his efforts some 800 new species of flowering plants, including trees, were imported into Europe. And one particular orchid that he discovered in

European collectors in South America around 1890, together with the collecting baskets they used for transporting orchids from their jungle habitats to the ports

South America was named *Miltoniopsis roezlii* in his honour.

### The lure of wealth ...

Europe was soon gripped by 'orchid fever' as wealthy aristocrats and *nouveaux riches* indulged their passion for exotic collections. They would pay large sums for newly discovered plants in a craze that was to last until the outbreak of World War I. Particularly novel or beautiful specimens would be offered for auction. The record for this was achieved at Sotheby's in London in 1903, when a specimen of *Odontoglossum crispum* went for an astronomical sum.

### ... and the inevitable consequences

Often only a few years passed between the discovery of a new orchid species and its extinction at the hands of overzealous collectors.

- The first tropical orchid to flower in Europe is said to have been a *Brassavola nodosa* (lady-of-the-night; see page 86) in 1615.
- In 1768 Sir Joseph Banks, who accompanied Capt. James Cook on his Pacific voyage in the 'Endeavour', collected the first orchids from the East Indies.
- Between 1854 and 1899, orchid growers created about 1,000 orchid hybrids.
- In 1899 as many as 100,000 specimens of *Odontoglossum crispum* were imported from Colombia and auctioned in Britain – an appalling case of overexploitation!
- In 1906 Henry Sander published the first *Sander's List of Orchid Hybrids* (see page 92). Ever since then it has remained the official publication for the registration of all orchid hybrids world-wide (now available on CD-ROM).

### Orchids as medicinal and spice plants

To the ancient Greeks, the testicle-shaped tubers of *Orchis* species (also native to this country) were a symbol of fertility and so came to be used as an aphrodisiac.

The best-known orchid to be used as a spice plant is vanilla (*Vanilla planifolia*; see page 37), which was used as far back as AD 1100 by the Incas of Cuzco in Peru. The spice is actually obtained from the fermented seed pods.

The first book on American medicines, the *Codex Badiano* published by Martin de la Cruz in 1552, refers to vanilla as an effective remedy against hysteria, fever, impotence and rheumatism. *Encyclia citrina* was recommended for infections, colds and sunstroke, and *Laelia autumnalis* and *Stanhopea hernandezii* (now called *S. tigrina*) for the much-dreaded dysentery.

## What is an orchid?

### The flower

It was the large, brightly coloured flowers of tropical

*The flower of* Cattleya loddigesii *from Brazil. The petals, sepals and lip are all clearly visible.*

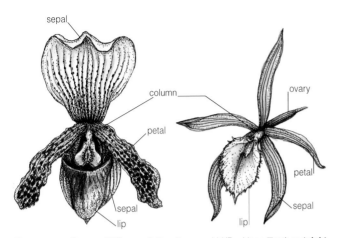

*The structure of two orchid flowers:* **left** *a slipper orchid* (Paphiopedilum) *and* **right** *a Brassavola*

It's actually extremely easy to remove pollen from the tip of the column of an orchid. A light touch with a pencil is sufficient to pollinate a plant artificially.

orchids that sparked off the first wave of orchid fever in Europe. Other aspects of the flowers are similarly of interest today. Take, for example, those flowers that resemble insects (such as our native fly and bee orchids; see page 36), or the diminutive size of some miniature orchid flowers, or the intensity of colour in the orchids of the cloud forests.

Most orchids have rather small flowers that are nonetheless interesting in colour or shape. Only relatively few genera bear the large, extremely attractive flowers that make them such ideal houseplants.

The orchid flower has a symmetrical design and is effectively divided into two parts. The underneath part of the flower is the **ovary**, which later develops into the **seed pod**. The upper part consists of three outer leaves – or **sepals** – and three inner leaves that are called **petals**.

The central petal always has an unusual shape. It is larger and thicker, and has a different colour from the other petals. It is called the **lip** (labellum). In some orchids, such as the appropriately named slipper orchid (*Paphiopedilum*), the lip is shaped like a slipper.

The surface of the lip is often characterised by fleshy growths. These ridges, plates and other marks are known as **callus tissue**.

The lip sometimes has a long growth at the back called the **spur**, where pollinating insects find nectar. As the flower develops from a bud, its stem turns through 180 degrees, bringing the lip to the bottom of the flower, where it then serves as a landing place for insects.

All orchids in the wild are pollinated by small creatures – mainly insects. In orchids the number of stamens is limited to two (or even one), and they are almost or completely fused with the stigma. The organ resulting from this fusion is called the **column**, and is typical of orchids. The pollen is found at the tip of the column, while the stigma forms the base, which means that orchids are unable to self-pollinate.

From a botanical point of view, orchids are one of the youngest plant families. The oldest fossils go back only some 15 million years, by contrast with other plant families with fossils going back as far as

9

*Coelogyne cristata is an orchid that is characterised by roundish, slightly wrinkled pseudobulbs, sympodial growth, visibly dried-up leaf sheaths or nodal leaves, and rhizomes.*

60–100 million years. It is generally assumed, therefore, that orchids are still very much in the process of evolution. One consequence of this is that the individual orchid genera are not properly 'fixed' and can be fairly easily crossed with each other to produce hybrid genera (see page 61). This characteristic is very much the exception among flowering plants.

If an orchid has pseudobulbs, this is a clear indication that it will enter a dormant state for at least part of the year.

## Pseudobulbs and tubers

The strange, bulbous formations that are found in many orchids have nothing to do with bulbs as such. They sometimes consist of thickened nodes in the stem, which may be round or elongated and of varying thickness; or alternatively they may be made up of several nodes that have become fused to form a single swelling. They may occur on any part of the shoot and are known as **pseudobulbs**, their main purpose being to store water and nutrients.

Swellings in the shoots that occur under the soil, such as in our native *Orchis* species, are similarly used as storage organs, but these are **tubers** and not pseudobulbs. The fact that the paired tubers of *Orchis* look rather like testicles (in Greek *orchis*, plural *orchides*) is what originally gave orchids their name.

There are usually one or two leaves at the tip of a pseudobulb. They vary in size and are soft and sometimes even fleshy. Some of them live through several growth periods, while others last only for a single season. Sometimes these nodal leaves are found all over the pseudobulb. Some pseudobulbs are wrapped in a single leaf sheath.

The section of stem linking pseudobulbs is called the **rhizome**. This is usually hard and woody, and may be short or long.

## The leaves

Orchid leaves have the same function as in all green plants: that of harnessing light to convert inorganic matter into organic matter in a process known as photosynthesis. Their structure is therefore typical of most leaves, though they vary in outward appearance. They may be round or elongated, soft or leathery, but the veins always run parallel. All orchid leaves, whether hard or soft, large or small, are adapted to the climatic conditions in the particular habitat where that orchid grows in the wild.

The leaves are normally arranged in two rows opposite one another along the shoot. However, many shoots have only one proper leaf, the other leaves being stunted and visible only as scale-like growths. On the other hand, some orchids are grown specifically for their leaves.

**Orchids with decorative leaves**

*Ludisia discolor* has dark-red, almost purple, leaves with yellow veins, and the flowers are also very beautiful. Most other orchids with ornamental leaves are difficult to look after. The leaves of some tropical species of slipper orchid (*Paphiopedilum*) may be mottled or have decorative vein patterns. Some have reddish leaves with lighter-coloured veins that reflect the light.

**Leaves as storage organs**

Some orchids such as the well-known moth orchid (*Phalaenopsis*) use their leaves for

storage. In habitats with strong light conditions, the leaves are reduced to cylindrical structures that provide for storage as well as photosynthesis.

**Orchids with unusual leaves**

There are a few very unusual orchids which are **saprophytic**, absorbing nutrients from decaying matter. These plants rarely if ever absorb these nutrients on their own, depending on the fungi with which they live in symbiosis. The leaves are either present only for short periods, or reduced to scale-like structures.

*Vanda is a typical example of a monopodial orchid. The shoot simply grows upwards, and the lower portion becomes bare of leaves as the shoot develops.*

Cattleya *grows sympodially – see the elongated pseudobulbs, the relatively large, dry leaf sheaths, the rhizome and parts of the aerial roots.*

**Sympodial or monopodial growth**

Orchids can be divided into two groups according to the way they grow, although there are a few transitional forms:

- Most orchids are **sympodial** in that they grow to form several shoots. A shoot finishes growing each year with an **apical bud**, and growth resumes the following year from a **lateral bud**. Thus sympodial orchids spread out in all directions – a pattern familiar to us from the various native species.

- Other orchids are known as **monopodial** because they grow as a single main shoot that carries on growing indefinitely. However, depending on the climatic conditions, it may enter a dormant period before resuming growth at a later stage.

11

*The aerial roots of a Dendrobium. The tips of the roots are green, while the rest of them is covered with a white layer called velamen that absorbs moisture from the air.*

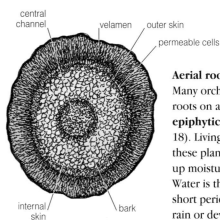

*A cross-section through an orchid root*

If the root grows, the rest of the orchid grows too. A sickly root can spell the end for the orchid. So all sickly roots should be removed, and if necessary the whole plant should be repotted.

Sympodial orchids produce flowers from apical or lateral buds, whereas monopodial plants will flower only from lateral buds.

## The roots

Orchid roots are different from those of most other plants. They are thicker on the outside, and white, grey or yellowish in colour, while the outer surface may be soft or very hard.

The roots of **terrestrial** orchids such as the slipper orchid have a downy covering of brown, yellow or white hairs. They branch out directly from the shoot, radiating from the base of the plant rather like the spokes of a wheel. The green tip of the root is the part that actually grows.

Orchid roots perform the usual tasks of absorbing water and nutrients, enabling the plant to breathe and anchoring it in position – but in orchids these roles are differently organised from the way they function in other plants. Indeed, some orchids can become so specialised in their way of life that the root is able take over some of the job of photosynthesis as well as absorbing nutrients and moisture.

## Aerial roots

Many orchids develop aerial roots on account of their **epiphytic** lifestyle (see page 18). Living on tree branches, these plants are unable to take up moisture from the soil. Water is thus available only for short periods in the form of rain or dew, at which point it must be absorbed and stored in the roots.

Aerial roots also perform other tasks – notably that of anchoring the plant to the host branch. If you try to remove an epiphytic orchid from its branch, you will inevitably damage the roots. Each root is firmly attached to the host, nestling tightly into the crevices. Later on, when a root has died, the remaining tissue still keeps the plant firmly anchored, effectively wiring it in position.

Special fungi known as mycorrhizae live on the roots, forming a symbiotic relationship with the orchid.

## Root structure

If you examine a root more closely, you will find that it is made up of several layers. The outer layer is the **velamen**, which consists mainly of dead cells that can fill up with water like a sponge. When dry, the velamen looks silvery in colour because the cells are filled with air. When it is wet, the chloroplasts (where photosynthesis takes place) in the underlying tissue show through the velamen layer, giving the root a greenish hue.

A layer of **permeable cells** forms the link to the centre of the root, through which the water and nutrients flow. Inside the velamen is an outer skin followed by the root bark and an internal skin – a firmer layer of cells that are similarly permeable.

Sometimes epiphytic roots happen to enter the soil, and when this happens they adapt accordingly. They become round instead of flat, and the velamen layer becomes much thinner. Among the more-or-less horizontally growing aerial roots, some of the thinner ones begin to grow vertically to form a kind of basket. This becomes a trap for discarded plant material, and for the waste and bodies of small creatures such as insects, which provide further nutrients.

Most **terrestrial orchids** grow in humus-rich soil – an open, very permeable substrate that is similar to loose woodland soil.

They too have velamen in their roots, which in turn affects the way they should be treated and maintained.

Yet another distinctive feature of orchids is that each root grows for only one season. After that it continues to function, however, and new roots form in the following season. But this does mean that damaged roots are unable to regenerate.

## World distribution of orchids

The orchid family (Orchidaceae) contains more species than any other family of flowering plants. Experts differ on the exact number of species, although there are generally thought to be at least 20,000 to 25,000, or perhaps even 30,000 altogether. No one knows for sure. Many species have been registered twice – hence the number of synonyms in the official register – while others have yet to be discovered.

Orchids can be found all over the world in almost every climatic zone, the only exceptions being arid deserts and polar zones.

*The number of orchid species occurring in the continents of the world*

## at a glance

- Orchids are no longer the preserve of the few, but they remain as fascinating as ever.

- There are more hybrids on the market than naturally occurring species.

- The orchid flower is similar to that of a lily, but typically has a noticeable lip.

- Many orchids have storage organs called pseudobulbs; they usually require a dormant period.

- The leaves are adapted to the environment, and may be soft or leathery.

- Orchids may grow either monopodially or sympodially.

- Most orchids develop aerial roots.

- Orchids grow in almost every part of the world, including the UK.

# Buying, planting and maintenance

Choosing the right orchid to buy for your home can make all the difference between success and failure. But then, provided you give your orchid the daily care it needs, it should flower for a long time.

## Buying orchids

In a visitor survey at a flower exhibition in 1998 where orchids were on sale, 36% of those who owned orchids had bought them from a flower shop, 34% from an orchid specialist and 21% from a garden centre. Ordering by post from an orchid specialist was a common method of purchase. Astonishingly, only 37% of the visitors surveyed did not have any orchids, while 41% possessed between one and five orchids and 20% owned more than five. The vast number of *Phalaenopsis* (moth orchids) sold is perhaps not surprising: in 1997 as many as four million were exported from the Netherlands alone.

As many as 57% of visitors surveyed thought that orchids weren't very difficult house-plants to look after, while only 38% had had bad experiences with them. Many failures would no doubt have been due to poor maintenance, but other orchids may well have failed simply because the wrong plant was bought in the first place. Such an avoidable mistake may be down to the vendor giving wrong or misleading care instructions. The sparse indications given on a small label may only serve to confuse – 'half shade, water sparingly' – while sometimes the plants are not fully identified.

Buying the right orchid makes a significant difference to the likelihood of success, though whether you buy a moth or a slipper orchid is very much a matter of personal taste.

### Points to note when buying

Look very carefully at whatever plants you decide to buy. Look out for any weaknesses and bear the following points in mind:

- You should know the full name of the orchid, or at least be able to find it out. Without this you will be unable to find the necessary information as to the correct position for the plant and the care requirements.

- Check the state of the leaves. Never buy an orchid with wilted or damaged leaves, or with sickly roots or visible pest damage – all of these are factors that will greatly reduce your chances of success.

- Heavy, wet soil can quickly lead to irreparable damage.

- It's easy to tell whether orchids have been well treated from the way they are presented. If the packing hasn't been removed, especially with *Phalaenopsis*, this leads quickly to *Botrytis* (grey mould) infection; and if plants are poorly presented or the panicles are broken, this suggests they haven't been treated with much care.

*◄ All white* Phalaenopsis *plants are descended from* Phalaenopsis amabilis. *This picture shows why* Phalaenopsis *is also called the moth orchid. The slipper orchid in the adjacent pot should similarly be kept warm.*

Never buy an orchid that isn't properly labelled, as you will have no means of finding out any further information about it.

Never buy an orchid that's standing in a draught. You won't see the effects of this until later, when dropping buds will be the least of your worries.

If the shop or garden centre is too cool, the buds may start dropping when you get the plant indoors. Transporting the plant home also requires careful consideration. A car may be cold in winter or overheated in

*Orchid exhibitions provide a wide choice of different plants, but this doesn't necessarily mean they will all be of good quality.*

summer. In winter you should insist on frost-proof packaging; several layers of newspaper should provide good protection. Plastic film should be rejected not only on environmental grounds but because it increases the risk of *Botrytis* infection.

You should never buy a plant with obvious faults, even if it's cheap. On the other hand, faded flowers on an otherwise healthy plant may mean it's cheaper to buy.

Plants with lots of buds carry a certain risk, because they are less likely to withstand the journey home. If most of the buds on a spray are already in flower, there's a reduced risk of buds dropping.

## Conservation issues

If you try to bring wild orchids home from abroad as holiday souvenirs, then you may get a nasty surprise when you go through Customs. Wild orchids are all protected species and it's illegal to import them into the UK. They will most likely be confiscated and you may well be fined too.

If you want to bring orchid plants back from a foreign holiday, you will need to have

the correct paperwork (see page 60 for further advice).

# Factors affecting growth

Warmth, light and humidity are all controllable factors, but 'green fingers' can't be bought at any price. They are the product of patience and observation.

## Light conditions

Like all green plants, orchids need light for photosynthesis. Tropical orchids are used to fairly similar light conditions throughout the year, although local conditions may vary.

Because orchids grow slowly, they wouldn't stand much chance in the tropics of growing on the ground, where they would be quickly stifled by faster-growing vegetation. This is why most tropical orchids are **epiphytic**, living on the branches of trees or shrubs. Some are even **lithophytic**, living on rocks. Depending on their light requirements, they may grow at the tip of a branch, inside the crown of a tree or even below a major branch.

Indoor light conditions are generally sufficient for an orchid's needs, and it normally

The leaves alone may provide clues about their light requirements that could have an influence on where you put the plants. Orchids with strong or leathery leaves might prefer a southern aspect, while those with soft leaves might do much better near a more northerly window.

*Plant communities grow better than single plants by helping each other out. Some plants provide shade, while others have large, leathery leaves that help conserve humidity. Orchids benefit similarly from 'communal living', especially with daylight lamps to enhance the growing conditions.*

temperature requirements for a particular plant. For practical purposes, gardeners classify plants into three main groups according to the greenhouse temperatures they require – **cold**, **temperate** and **warm** – flourishes where other tropical plants flourish. Where lighting is reduced – in winter, for example – special daylight lamps can be used to help make up the deficit.

## Temperature

Persian violets (*Exacum affine*) will tolerate cooler temperatures than African violets (*Saint-paulia*). Some orchids need to be treated like African violets, and others like Persian violets. So it's essential to know the

| Gardeners' temperature classification for orchids | | | |
|---|---|---|---|
| Average recommended indoor temperatures in Celsius and in Fahrenheit | | | |
| **Month** | **Cold** | **Temperate** | **Warm** |
| January | 8–12/46–54 | 15–18/59–64 | 18–24/64–75 |
| February | 9–13/48–55 | 16–18/61–64 | 19–24/66–75 |
| March | 9–13/48–55 | 16–20/61–68 | 19–24/66–75 |
| April | 10–14/50–57 | 16–20/61–68 | 20–25/68–77 |
| May | 11–14/52–57 | 18–21/64–70 | 20–25/68–77 |
| June | 12–15/54–59 | 18–21/64–70 | 20–28/68–82 |
| July | 12–15/54–59 | 18–21/64–70 | 20–28/68–82 |
| August | 12–15/54–59 | 18–21/64–70 | 20–28/68–82 |
| September | 10–14/50–57 | 16–20/61–68 | 19–24/66–75 |
| October | 9–13/48–55 | 16–20/61–68 | 19–24/66–75 |
| November | 8–12/46–54 | 15–18/59–64 | 18–24/64–75 |
| December | 8–12/46–54 | 15–18/59–64 | 18–24/64–75 |

and much the same principle applies to room temperatures.

The table on the previous page gives the recommended room and greenhouse temperatures in both Celsius and Fahrenheit. You don't need to follow them slavishly, as orchids are able to adapt to some extent and will tolerate some variation. Orchids are after all no different from many other houseplants, hating cold or draughts, burning in the sun and suffering in the shade.

## How orchids live

Orchids may be divided into two main groups:

- **terrestrial orchids** that live on the ground
- **epiphytic orchids** that live on the branches of other plants.

The great majority of orchids that are grown as houseplants are of the epiphytic kind.

If the soil is sticky and covered with moss or algae, then it's poorly aerated. This problem can often occur when there is too much moisture.

Oncidium *in its native Brazilian habitat. As an epiphyte it has aerial roots, pseudobulbs and leathery leaves, and of course it needs to hold on tight!*

## Epiphytic orchids

Orchids aren't the only tropical plants that grow as epiphytes. The same is true of many bromeliads and ferns. Lack of light on the ground is the main reason why they have colonised the branches.

Epiphytes have many interesting adaptations to their 'aerial' environment, including aerial roots that do more than just hold on tight, succulent leaves and various storage organs (see page 10). However, epiphytes are not parasites, because they don't draw nutrients from the plants they have colonised.

### Recreating the jungle at home

How can you enable such plants to survive in your home? The most natural and obvious

solution might be to provide an epiphytic location, whether on a branch or a piece of wood, or in a wooden or plastic basket. However, this will only work if the air and light conditions, temperature and humidity are kept exactly as they are in the tropics – and this is only possible in a greenhouse or an orchid case (see pages 49 ff.).

### The right soil is essential

It's still possible to create the right conditions in a pot using a specialist substrate, whether on a windowsill or in a greenhouse or conservatory. But the substrate must fulfil certain important criteria.

It must be particularly open and airy (see pages 21 ff.). As the roots need plenty of fresh air in order to function properly, the soil must never be allowed to become compacted. The other vital ingredient for growing epiphytes is **soft water** with a low salt content.

### The dormancy period

All orchids with pseudobulbs – and that includes most epiphytes – need a period of rest. They use this adaptation in their natural habitat to survive periods of difficult conditions, when they scarcely grow at all.

Dormancy runs independently of our own seasons, and lasts until the growing season begins. Many orchids rest for as long as five months, while others need only three or four weeks at the most.

## Terrestrial orchids

Originally all orchids grew on the ground. It was only poor light and competition from faster-growing plants that drove some of them up into the branches. Although terrestrial orchids grow naturally on the ground, they still prefer open, humus-rich soils in woodlands, hedgerows or meadows.

### Which orchids are terrestrial?
The best-known of the tropical terrestrials are from the genera *Paphiopedilum* (slipper orchids) and *Cymbidium* (although not all of these are terrestrial). Our native orchids are all terrestrial, as are the Mediterranean and many mountain-growing species.

### The characteritics of terrestrial orchids
Terrestrial orchids have better access to groundwater than epiphytic orchids, and nutrients are more consistently available

to them. Like epiphytic orchids, they usually enter a period of dormancy, which may be very long in the case of those with tubers. Other terrestrials such as tropical slipper orchids only need to rest if there is a drought or if there is a drop in temperature.

Because the roots of terrestrial orchids are better protected by the soil, they generally cope better in the short term with adverse factors such as wind, light or dryness, and the roots have adapted accordingly.

However, because they come from a more equable environment than epiphytic orchids, they generally cope less well with extreme conditions.

### Looking after terrestrial orchids
The soil should never be allowed to dry out, but neither should it be allowed to become waterlogged. Nutrient requirements may increase in the growing season. Roots should only be removed if they are rotten or damaged.

In contrast to tropical orchids, which grow in regions with a relatively unchanging climate, many terrestrial orchids come from areas with big seasonal changes. This means that the

Cymbidium tracyanum *is a terrestrial orchid that comes originally from the mountains of Myanmar (Burma) in southern Asia. As a houseplant it likes cool, well-lit conditions. It can be placed in the garden during the summer.*

period of dormancy is more marked, whether through drought or through winter cold, as the leaves drop and growth stops completely.

Otherwise there is little difference in terms of maintenance requirements, except that finer ingredients are needed for the substrate.

Terrestrial orchids of British origin may also be grown in the garden, although it's not always that simple. They are usually on sale at specialised outlets. Moreover, all our native orchids are protected species, so you should always ask your dealer for proof of origin.

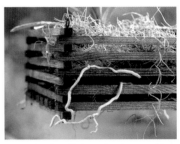

*Whether you choose a plant pot or a wooden basket will depend on the prevailing conditions (humidity) and the time available. Wooden baskets dry out more quickly indoors, but are ideal for greenhouses. Transparent pots allow aerial roots to photosynthesise as they do in the wild.*

## Plant pots and containers

The container is effectively an orchid's home, while the substrate can be compared to the furniture. It follows from this that the plant won't feel properly settled until its home is well furnished.

Rossioglossum grande, *also known as* Odontoglossum grande, *in a commercially available container. Shallow bowls like this one are well suited to the requirements of epiphytic orchids.*

◄ *This picture shows clearly why* Rossioglossum grande *has become generally known as the clown orchid.*

There used to be special orchid pots – clay pots with large holes in the sides – and there were extra-tall pots for *Cymbidium* orchids because these plants develop so many roots that they quickly fill up their container, pushing the plant out at the top.

These days there are special containers for epiphytic orchids consisting of baskets made of wood and plastic. These are not really necessary, though epiphytes do prefer a shallow container as the roots tend to spread horizontally.

Nowadays, plastic containers have generally won out over clay pots. In a clay pot the moisture continually evaporates outwards, cooling the soil and leaving salt deposits that may damage the roots.

A plastic pot, on the other hand, requires less watering and is easy to clean. It may often be too lightweight for tall plants, but a little gravel in the bottom will usually improve its stability. Only high-quality plastics should be used.

- Shallow bowls with plenty of drainage make ideal containers for orchids.

- Other good candidates are the wooden baskets and wire baskets that are used for water plants, because they allow plenty of air to get to the roots. You can always put in netting to prevent the finer elements of the substrate from getting washed away. The best solution is the plastic netting used for storing fruit.

- Pots, bowls or baskets made of cork bark – which are available from florists – can also look extremely attractive.

# Growing mediums

Whenever you buy a ready-made orchid compost, you should always check on its composition and compare it with that of others on the market.

All orchids need a loose, open mixture, although the exact composition required has been the subject of dispute ever since the first tropical orchids were brought to Europe.

It is generally agreed, however, that all the ingredients should be relatively coarse so that they won't easily become compacted. They should also be slightly acid and contain little or no salt. On the other hand,

there is no substrate that is equally suitable for all orchids or for all orchid growers.

## Natural materials

At one time the basic ingredients for orchid compost used to be fern roots, *Sphagnum* moss and beech leaves.

The fern roots came from species that are now protected, such as royal fern (*Osmunda regalis*). Fern roots are sometimes still available, but they come from tropical tree ferns that are similarly protected, and their sale is therefore strictly controlled. So before buying any fern roots you should find out where they came from.

**Peat** varies from the more fibrous forms that are generally used in gardening to the darker

*Orchid compost, coconut chips and bark, with polystyrene chips in the foreground for improving drainage. The aerial roots of an orchid are clearly visible inside the transparent plastic pot.*

*An orchid compost with polystyrene chips that help the soil to 'breathe'. They may occupy up to 30% of the substrate.*

forms that are used for burning. The use of peat is nowadays very controversial, and while orchid compost has probably not yet been responsible for the loss of a whole peat bog, it's best not to use peat if at all possible.

Other ingredients used include:

- the **bark** of pines and Douglas firs, obtained from older, fully grown trees

Find a growing medium that suits your purposes. If you tend to overwater, use coarser materials. If the opposite is true, it may be worth using a little extra peat to prevent the soil from drying out. If you're a beginner, you should start with a ready-made substrate.

- **coir** – a fibrous waste material from coconut products.

Some orchid enthusiasts use gravel, garden compost and loam as additional ingredients, although this is mainly for terrestrial orchids.

## Minerals and synthetic materials

These have often proved to be good substitutes for expensive natural products. Bear in mind that orchids growing in synthetic mediums are supposed to tolerate larger doses of fertiliser if faster growth is required. On the other hand, faster growth also makes for softer tissues that are more susceptible to infections.

Various foam materials (including foam rubber) are normally used. Perhaps the best-known such material is **polystyrene chips**. These help to keep the soil well aired. They can, however, create problems in combination with peat. Especially during the latter part of the growing season, the soil becomes sticky and compacted, and the aerial roots begin to suffocate and die. This can even happen if you do everything correctly, and it can only be prevented by means of frequent

| Factor | Peat |
|---|---|
| **pH value** | very low |
| **Salt content** | low |
| **Nutrients** | very low |
| **Water capacity** | good |
| **Air capacity** | good |
| **Effect on plants** | very good |
| **Stability** | very good |
| **Effect on environment** | controversial |
| **Notes** | good buffer, almost sterile |
| **Significance** | a potentially useful additional ingredient |

and regular transplanting.

Other useful potting materials include **perlite**, **pumice** and **clay pellets**, all of which can be recommended if they are used in the right proportions.

One material that works well without any added ingredients is **rockwool**, which is produced from molten rock and maintains its structure for a long

## The characteristics of various potting ingredients

| Bark | Clay pellets | Coir | *Sphagnum* | Fern | Garden compost | Polystyrene chips | Rockwool |
|---|---|---|---|---|---|---|---|
| variable | neutral | medium | low | low | high | neutral | neutral |
| low | low to medium | variable | low to medium | low | medium | none | none |
| medium to low | low to medium | low | low | low | medium to high | none | none |
| satisfactory | very good | poor to very good | very good | very good | good | low | very good |
| very good | very good | good to very good | very good | very good | good | very good | good |
| very good | very good | good | good | good | very good | very good | |
| very good | very good | very good | satisfactory | very good | good | very good | very good |
| very good | good | controversial | controversial | controversial | very good | controversial | controversial |
| reduces disease, difficult to regulate nitrogen | weighs a lot, Seramis only if watering can be sufficiently regulated | no buffering, best conditions for epiphytes, available as chips | kills bacteria and fungi | natural surrounding for orchids | only for terrestrial orchids | most important additional ingredient | only to be used under strict supervision |
| used in nearly all substrates | additional ingredient | important | important in epiphytes for rooting from pseudobulbs | unimportant because rarely available legally | important for terrestrial orchids | for all substrates | for professional gardeners |

time. This material is also cheap, sterile and contains no nutrients, which means that the plants can be fed and watered in controlled amounts. But they then need to be checked regularly, as the effects of excess or insufficient nutrients will be more quickly felt. This isn't a good medium for amateur orchid growers.

The opposite is true of **Seramis**. These are special clay pellets that even out the effects of mistakes in treatment (see pages 34 ff.).

Clay pellets in general have many positive features: they retain not only moisture and nutrients, but also oxygen – and they are also structurally stable (see pages 32 ff.).

Plants in sticky, peaty mixtures should be immediately repotted and any further stress should be avoided. You may have to reckon without flowers for the initial period.

## Tried-and-tested orchid composts

| Mixture 1 for epiphytic orchids | Mixture 2 for epiphytic orchids | Mixture 1 for terrestrial orchids | Mixture 2 for terrestrial orchids |
|---|---|---|---|
| 1 part beech leaves | 3 parts peat | 1 part beech leaves | 3 parts peat |
| 2 parts wood shavings | 2 parts bark | 1 part coarse peat | 2 parts polystyrene chips |
| 1 part coir (chips) | 2 parts polystyrene chips | 1 part fine, fibrous peat | 2 parts loam |
| 1 part pine bark | 1 part clay pellets | 1 part clay pellets or loam | 2 parts clay pellets |
| 1 part *Sphagnum* | | 1 part bark | |

**Mixture 1 for epiphytic orchids**

**Added fertiliser per litre volume**
3 g chalk
2 g hoof and horn
0.5 g trace-element fertiliser

**Notes**
You can increase the proportion of coir to bind the mixture.
For pots add 0.25 g complete fertiliser.

**Mixture 2 for epiphytic orchids**

**Added fertiliser per litre volume**
4 g chalk
2 g hoof and horn
0.5 g complete fertiliser
0.5 g trace-element fertiliser

**Notes**
Universal mixture remains stable for two years.

**Mixture 1 for terrestrial orchids**

**Added fertiliser per litre volume**
3 g chalk
0.5 g complete fertiliser
0.5 g trace-element fertiliser

**Notes**
You can use finer ingredients for some orchids (e.g. *Paphiopedilum*).

**Mixture 2 for terrestrial orchids**

**Added fertiliser per litre volume**
Same as for mixture 1

**Notes**
Suitable for *Cymbidium*, *Zygopetalum*

Whereas beech leaves once used to be an important ingredient of orchid compost, they are little used nowadays. Because they are always collected the previous autumn, they won't have decayed very much and will improve the structure of the substrate. They also provide a slow supply of nutrients over the long term, which is just right for an amateur grower.

*Orchids in mass production – here seen on a potting machine – are commonplace nowadays.*

# Repotting

Like all slow-growing plants, orchids only rarely need repotting. They should only be repotted:

- if there's no space left in the pot for new growth
- if the surface of the substrate is sticky or is covered with algae
- if the substrate has decomposed or the roots are rotting.

Always repot when the first new growth begins (e.g. when a heart-shaped leaf forms on *Phalaenopsis*; see page 39).

## Preparation

- Prepare the growing medium and moisten if necessary. (If you decide to use peat and it's very dry, a touch of washing-up liquid will help the water to soak in.)
- Water your orchids three days before repotting, adding fertiliser for healthy plants.
- Check your plants for any evidence of pests, and deal with these before repotting.
- Lay out your tools ready: a sharp knife or secateurs, a fine atomiser, a watering can, plastic foil, and also string,

wire and canes; polystyrene chips for drainage; gravel for stabilising small pots.

## Procedure

- Ease the orchid out of its old pot, taking care not to damage the roots. Carefully remove any loose soil – don't pull at it!
- Cut off all damaged or rotting roots, always cutting smoothly and cleanly to avoid crushing the tissues.
- Cut off all rotting or damaged leaves, flowers and buds.
- Dividing plants. With sympodial plants, always leave at least three healthy pseudobulbs, and divide at the branching points in the rhizome. It is possible to take cuttings from monopodial plants, or from those with elongated pseudobulbs with plenty of nodes.
- Always choose new pots that are large enough to accommodate at least two new shoots (pseudobulbs). When repotting monopodial orchids, you should use a pot at least three sizes bigger than the previous one (e.g. repot from a 10-cm pot to a 13-cm pot).

- When you're fixing an epiphytic orchid to a mount, make sure you bind it firmly, using a little soft substrate (e.g. *Sphagnum*). In a pot, if roots are missing, use wire hooks as a substitute; place a cane in the pot and add a drainage layer.
- Place the orchid in the pot. With a sympodial plant, place it so that the last shoot touches the rim. Place small plants or monopodials in the centre of the pot. Add the substrate and press it down just enough to stop the plant from wobbling.
- Only water the pot if the substrate is dry (use the finger test; see page 27).
- Find a position that is protected from direct sunlight. Use foil or fleece to prevent evaporation. Don't water for the first few weeks – just spray your plants.
- Protect new growth from slugs, aphids, scale insects or rot.
- Once the new roots have formed, remove the foil. First use a high-nitrogen fertiliser, then after two or three months feed regularly with an ordinary fertiliser.

**1** *Ease the orchids carefully out of the old pot. This will be easier if the substrate is damp. Check the old substrate for pests. Remove all loose remnants, but be careful not to pull at anything.*

**2** *Now cut off all visibly damaged or sickly (brown, soggy or dry) roots with a sharp pair of secateurs. Cut cleanly to avoid crushing.*

**3** *Having chosen your new pot, you should also remove any healthy roots that won't fit in the pot without being bent or broken.*

**4** *Fill the pot with new substrate up to about 1 cm below the rim. If it's a Phalaenopsis, hold it in the centre of the pot, with the roots radiating out close to the surface and almost touching the side of the pot. Place sympodial orchids so that two shoots (pseudobulbs) come up to the rim of the pot.*

**5** *Place the plant in the new pot and put in a drainage layer (polystyrene chips or gravel). Now place more substrate carefully around the roots, with the coarser elements below. Avoid crushing the roots at all costs.*

**6** *Finally, press down the substrate carefully, tapping the pot gently to fill up any hollows, and do a final check.*

# Watering correctly

Correct watering is vital to your orchids' success.

Very few plants die of thirst, while some 90% are effectively drowned by too much watering. Overwatering deprives the roots of oxygen, with the result that they suffocate and the plant becomes starved.

The orchid depends on water being channelled up from the roots. If the roots are broken or damaged, they can't fulfil this task, even if there is enough water available.

In general, orchids should only be watered when the substrate is really dry.

## Water quality

Orchid growth is influenced by the water quality. The main factor here, apart from acidity, is the **hardness** of the water. You can ask your local water supplier about the hardness of your tap water. If you ask for it to be given in Clarks, you can use the following conversion:

0–3.5 = soft
3.5–7.0 = moderately soft
7.0–14.0 = slightly hard
14.0–21.0 = moderately hard
21.0–31.5 = hard
over 31.5 = very hard

Orchids need soft water. Hard water leads to unsightly chalky deposits on the leaves and flowers.

In the absence of rainwater or suitable soft water from a tap, well or spring, many orchid enthusiasts resort to various purification methods. There are a number of different solutions available on the market, all of them involving various physical or chemical means and devices.

However, even a coffee machine should be sufficient to do the trick, and will provide you with water which, while not distilled, will certainly be softer than water coming straight from the tap.

## Finger test

The finger test has always been the most reliable way of deciding whether you need to water. If the substrate feels cool and damp to the touch, then you shouldn't water. Because the substrate holds very little water, make sure you feel it carefully to be certain.

- Even if the leaves are wilting, don't water if the substrate feels damp.

- If the substrate is old and compacted, it needs less watering.

- Correct watering is easier with hydroculture, Seramis or other methods (see pages 32 ff.).

- The water you use should be at the same temperature as the ambient temperature of the room.

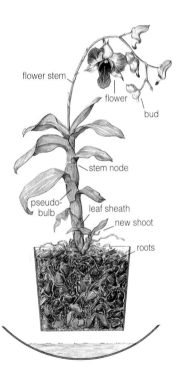

flower stem
flower
bud
stem node
pseudo-bulb
leaf sheath
new shoot
roots

**Watering correctly**

*An open substrate is the prerequisite for healthy roots. The right amount of water is vital to the health of the plant – too much and you will have wilted flowers, leaves and pseudobulbs.*

*Use soft water that is at room temperature. If you use tap water, leave it to stand to allow any chlorine to dissipate. Spread the water evenly over the surface of the substrate.*

about 55–80% for orchids growing indoors.

High humidity is no substitute for moist substrate, but neither can a moist substrate compensate for low humidity levels. You need both.

The best method to increase the humidity levels is to use a **window trough**. This is a shallow trough filled with a layer of pumice, lava or clay pellets in the bottom. The idea is to put water in the bottom, not quite covering the filling. The water surface is then allowed to evaporate and thus humidify the surrounding air. The process can be further enhanced by the presence of a central heating radiator, often located immediately below a windowsill, or by the sunshine streaming in.

## Humidity

The air around your orchids needs to be kept humid, as this is the only way that epiphytic plants can survive in the wild, given the small amounts of water and nutrients available to them (orchids grow fairly slowly in the wild). High humidity will also help to protect your orchids from too much sunlight.

The right humidity levels are easier to achieve in a cool room than in a warm room, and easier in a greenhouse than indoors. It would be wrong to specify a particular humidity level for all orchids, but in general you should aim for

*Misting systems have proved very successful, though these are only possible in a greenhouse. The water droplets are extremely fine, minimising the risk of damage to the plants, and in summer they help cool the air. Misting systems can be set up to run automatically.*

Another very good way of improving humidity indoors is to have other plants with large, soft leaves that give off moisture, such as bird's nest fern (*Asplenium nidus*), *Schefflera*, *Philodendron*, rubber plant (*Ficus elastica*) or *Calathea*.

useful. However, room humidifiers are expensive items to buy, and they need to be checked and topped up at regular intervals.

*A window trough will provide the necessary humidity indoors. This particular one contains (from left to right):* Paphiopedilum *(slipper orchid),* × Odontonia, Cymbidium *and* Rossioglossum grande *(clown orchid).*

Masdevallia coccinea *comes from the cloud forests of Colombia and Peru, where it grows at altitudes of 8,000–10,000 ft (2,400–3,000 m).*

Using one of these troughs can increase the humidity in the air surrounding the plants by as much as 30%. It also serves the further function of catching any excess water.

**Electrical humidifiers** and hand misters can also be very

# Feeding orchids

Orchids may be among the most self-contained of plants, but they still need nutrients, and they have specific nutrient requirements.

Apart from water and carbon dioxide, the **primary nutrients** they require are nitrogen, phosphorus and potassium, followed by the **secondary nutrients** sulphur, calcium and magnesium, and a number of **trace elements** including iron, manganese, copper and zinc.

Epiphytes have no problem with access to air, but more difficulty with obtaining water and nutrients, for which they use their aerial roots and to a certain extent their leaves.

In the wild, any available nutrients need to be absorbed quickly. They include nitrogen-rich water from thunderstorms, which runs down the bark of the host trees, picking up dust and nutrients in the process, including products from the decomposition of plants and small animals. All of these elements are only available for a short time.

In general, however, orchids are modest in their requirements, and will if anything be damaged by too much feeding.

## Feed moderately but regularly

Growth is limited by whatever nutrient is available in the smallest quantity – the so-called minimum factor. This one nutrient may be vital to the orchid's success. The lack of one nutrient can't be compensated for by the excess of another.

Any deficits don't always show themselves immediately, and may be difficult to recognise. Because orchids grow slowly, there may be a long interval between cause and effect. This means that prevention is better than cure, and that regular measured doses of fertiliser are preferable to a single concentrated dose of one particular nutrient.

The roots are mainly responsible for absorbing the nutrients, which means that poor growth may be due primarily to damaged roots rather than to a shortage of nutrients.

Nutrients in orchid substrates are available in a variety of different forms. Some of them are water-soluble, which means they can be accessed immediately after watering. In the case of orchid substrates, these are usually only available as either

*Zygopetalum hybrids are descended from species that came originally from Brazil and Peru. In winter they need a minimum temperature of around 12°C (54°F), so are not the best choice for indoor plants.*

basic or supplementary inorganic feeds. Other nutrients may be attached to humus or other minerals in the soil, and may, for example, need to be broken down by acids or micro-organisms before the plant can absorb them. The fewer nutrients available in the substrate, the more will need to be added in fertiliser.

### The right pH value

The pH value of soil indicates whether it is acidic or alkaline. A pH of 7 means the soil is neutral, while over 7 means it's alkaline and under 7 means it's acidic. Orchids prefer a pH of between 4.5 and 5.5, which means a weakly acid soil.

The pH of very acid substrates such as peat can be raised with **chalk**. Water with a high chalk content can have a similarly beneficial effect on very acid substrates. The right pH level is essential for nutrients to be properly absorbed.

### Orchid fertilisers

There is a wide range of orchid feeds available from a variety of manufacturers, but all of them have been specially designed to cater for the nutritional requirements of orchids. They should normally be added every third time you water, or according to the manufacturers' instructions. You should always measure the dose exactly.

*There is a wide choice of ready-made orchid feeds available today. They vary in composition and also in price.*

*Paphiopedilum 'Supersuk' is a magnificent hybrid that came from the crossing of three wild species:* P. lawrenceanum, P. mastersianum *and* P. sukhakulii.

During the growing season, use an orchid feed with nitrogen, phosphorus and potassium in the ratio 2:1:1, switching to 1:1:1 towards the end of the growth period. Bark or leaf-and-wood substrates need higher nitrogen levels – 4:1:1. You should be able to find the right combination among the fertilisers on offer.

Twice a year, at the beginning and at the end of the growth period, you should add an extra dose of trace elements. Your garden centre or orchid specialist should be able suggest a trace-element fertiliser or an orchid feed rich in trace elements.

Chalk (calcium carbonate) should be added at least twice a year in a dose of one teaspoonful (5 ml) per 10-cm pot, with further doses as necessary.

**Organic feeds** depend for their uptake on living organisms in the soil that can break them down into a form that can be absorbed. This means that organic feeds should only be used in conjunction with an organic substrate.

To prevent the orchids being damaged by any chemicals from the pot materials or the glaze, make sure the outer pot is waterproof and acid-resistant. It's best to use pots specifically intended for hydroculture, which are usually made of plastic. There is a wide choice of sizes and shapes available.

# Orchids in hydroculture

Some orchid growers have been using hydroponics or hydroculture for centuries. Hydroculture, like Seramis, only makes for better watering – all the other factors that influence growth remain unchanged, and pests aren't particularly affected if plants are growing in hydroculture or Seramis.

The simplest system of hydroculture consists of an inner and an outer pot. The inner pot contains clay pellets and a water-level indicator. The plant is also accommodated in the inner pot, while the outer pot contains water and a fertiliser cartridge if required.

## Equipment and technique

The inside pot is made of plastic and has a moulded recess to accommodate the water-level indicator, with a further recess if this is needed for a fertiliser cartridge. You need to check that the water-level indicator is the correct one for the size of the pot, otherwise it will give the wrong reading. The outer pot can be of any suitable size.

The **water-level indicator** is the most important element of hydroculture. It consists of a plastic tube with a red indicator that is moved up and down by a small float on the water surface. It is attached to the inner pot so that it extends down to the bottom of the outer pot below the water surface. As the water level rises, the indicator rises too so that you can read off the water level. The tube is also calibrated to show a minimum, an optimum and a maximum level, which means that you can tell exactly when you need to add water.

## Things to note

Orchids are particularly suited to hydroculture for two reasons. The first of these is the substrate, which is structurally firm; the clay pellets also contain a lot of oxygen and hold plenty of water.

The second reason is the fact that you can check the humidity using the water-level indicator. However, orchids in hydroculture need to be treated differently from other plants (see below).

Another important thing to note is that you should only convert your orchids to hydro-

The water-level indicator can of course only be useful if it's working properly. There have been cases where a water-level indicator has been blocked by a foreign body and stuck at a particular level, so that the plants were continually being over- or underwatered. Such a situation can come about when plant roots grow into the tube or salts precipitate out onto the float and prevent it from moving.

*Orchids in hydroculture. In this special form of orchid culture, it's important to achieve a harmony between plant and pot. You should therefore only use pots made of inert porcelain or plastic.*

culture when the plants have just begun to grow, i.e. when they've just begun to put out new roots, leaves or shoots.

## Converting orchids to hydroculture

- Always use clean pots, if necessary sterilising them beforehand using a suitable sterilising agent. Always use new clay pellets, or else sterilise them in the oven at 250°C (480°F).
- Clay pellets come in different sizes. You should use 14–16-mm pellets for fully grown plants; otherwise smaller pellets should be used. First wet the pellets in clean tap water.
- Remove the orchid from the old substrate in lukewarm water. Remove all damaged or rotting roots.
- Place the plant in a hydroculture pot of about the same size as the old one – and definitely no more than 5 cm larger.
- Hold the plant at the same height as in the old pot, and carefully add the pellets, taking great care not to crush any of the roots.
- If necessary, tie the plant to a cane to keep it stable; it shouldn't be allowed to wobble during the growth phase.
- Don't add any water at first. For the first three weeks a fine spray is sufficient – several times a day if necessary. A

clear plastic bag around the orchid will raise the humidity and help growth.

- After three weeks, add water for the first time and begin feeding.
- Orchids with thick, leathery leaves such as *Cymbidium* and *Phalaenopsis* can easily succumb to root rot despite the best care and attention. But because it's easier to check the roots in hydro-culture, it's possible to deal with the problem. If the roots start to rot, you should repeat the whole repotting procedure again.

The correct temperature and light conditions, as well as

With orchids in hydroculture, the water level shouldn't be allowed to reach maximum, and should be kept between the optimum and minimum levels. Don't water until the water level has sunk to minimum. The only exception is if you have to go on holiday during the growing season, when you may fill it (only once!) to the maximum level – it will usually last three weeks.

dormancy periods, need to be observed just as carefully with hydroculture as with other forms of culture.

For example, orchids growing in a cold greenhouse should not be watered during the resting phase. Slow-release fertilisers (using a fertiliser cartridge) are only suitable for fully rooted plants. Orchids are generally better suited to liquid feeds or special orchid fertilisers.

## Seramis and other special cultures

Apart from hydroculture, a number of other artificial culture methods have been tried out on orchids, from self-watering pots and polystyrene chips to a variety of plastic foams. All of them have one aim in common: that of making watering easier and preventing overwatering.

Self-watering containers usually involve the use of a wick made of cotton or nylon fibres that runs from the bottom of the water container into the substrate. The water creeps slowly into the substrate by means of capillary action. The water container takes the form

Dendrobium *Stardust 'Chyomi' – a cultivar of* D. nobile *– growing in Seramis culture. The water-level indicator helps greatly, but is no substitute for green fingers.*

of a tank or an outer pot, depending on the particular system that is being used.

### Seramis as an orchid substrate

Seramis is a special form of burnt clay with open pores. It is highly aerated and can store a large amount of water, making it of special interest to orchid growers. The water becomes well distributed throughout the substrate.

The manufacturers of Seramis recommend that plants should

**1** When transplanting to Seramis, first ease the plant gently from the old container. Remove any loose substrate, and if necessary cut open the root ball as for an ordinary substrate.

**3** Choose the new pot on the basis of the size of the newly trimmed roots. The remaining old substrate should make up only a third of the new Seramis culture.

**2** If there is very little soil left, you should only remove the sickly roots and transplant horizontal roots together with the plant.

**4** Finally, install the water-level indicator. Check it's working correctly and keep checking it at regular intervals.

the plant into the Seramis. It's therefore better to follow a procedure similar to that for hydroculture (see pages 33–34).

- It's safest to transplant at the beginning of the growth period.

- Remove all damaged roots, using a sharp knife to avoid crushing the tissues.

- Don't wash the old substrate out; simply top up with Seramis.

- You should choose a smaller pot for orchids than the manufacturers generally specify. However, the specified proportions of one part substrate to two parts Seramis generally applies to orchids too.

- The water-level indicator is only helpful with orchids during the growing season. In any case, you should check it regularly to make sure it's working correctly.

- Follow the watering and feeding procedures appropriate to the particular species, including the requisite dormant period.

*Phalaenopsis* and *Paphiopedilum* have both proved to be particularly successful in Seramis.

be transferred together with their root balls. But this only works with orchids if the old substrate is firmly structured, the roots are healthy and the root ball hangs together at all. Orchids tend to be sold in peaty, unstructured substrates. The roots are often damaged and rot is easily transferred with

**35**

# Propagation methods

Orchid propagation may often require the assistance of insects, chemicals, and knives or secateurs.

## Propagation by seed

Most orchids are pollinated by insects, but they have a number of unusual ways of achieving this end.

The strategy adopted by our native fly and bee orchids (*Ophrys*) is also common in the tropics: they attract insects by

Ophrys lutea *is a Mediterranean relative of our native bee orchid* (O. apifera) *and fly orchid* (O. insectifera). *The flowers mimic certain female insects, attracting the corresponding males to copulate and thus pollinate them. This terrestrial orchid may sometimes be sold as a garden plant.*

offering them the prospect of sex. The flowers mimic the females of various bees, wasps, flies etc. The disguise is so effective that males of the species land on the flowers and attempt to copulate with them. They pick up pollen in the process, which they deposit during their 'foreplay' on the next flower.

This is a trick commonly used by orchids to propagate themselves. Scent is just as important as sight, because these flowers also imitate the pheromones that the female insects produce. This has even been proved experimentally with *Ophrys* species, which produce a scent made up of as many as 27 different ingredients. What is more, as soon as an orchid has been pollinated, it stops producing the imitation pheromone.

Other orchids use a whole variety of strategies, including sweet-tasting nectars and traps (such as that of the slipper orchid), to persuade insects to pollinate them. Each particle of pollen is equipped with a sticky disc so that it sticks to the insect that touches it; some flowers even contain a sophisticated mechanism that shoots the pollen at the insect. When the

insect visits the next flower of the same species, it leaves the pollen on the stigma. Once pollination is completed, the seed begins to develop in the ovary (seed capsule).

The seed ripens in the ovary over a period of up to 20 months. Orchid seed is extremely small, and there may be as many as three million seeds in a single capsule (with *Cattleya*, for example). Each seed weighs on average only 0.005 mg. Once the capsule is ripe, it releases the seed on the wind, preferably from an open, windblown position so that the plant can spread as far as possible.

Not every seed produces an orchid. But if a seed reaches a place on the bark of a tree, it first attempts to gain a strong foothold. It takes in moisture and often forms spiral-shaped 'fingers' that hook into the bark like wire.

Orchid propagation so far has been little different from that of many other plants, except perhaps for the windswept location. But from this point onwards the orchid's existence becomes dependent on certain root fungi that form a symbiotic relationship with the new roots. The fungi are in fact absent

Vanilla is a spice that is obtained from the seed capsules (pods) of Vanilla planifolia. The ripe pods are harvested, dried and fermented.

Vanilla planifolia is the plant from which our familiar vanilla pods come. Originally found in the West Indies and Central America, it is now grown in plantations throughout the tropics.

from 99% of seedlings, which then go on to die. The fungi supply important nutrients to the plant. They penetrate specific layers of the roots, where they are eventually digested.

Now that we know which substances the fungi provide, it has become possible to bring the seeds in contact with the fungi in a test tube. Thus the laboratory has become today's orchid nursery – for garden orchids at least.

The time taken for an orchid embryo to turn into a fully grown plant varies according to genus and species, but it may be as long as 10 years – in the case of our native lady's slipper (*Cypripedium calceolus*), for example.

## Vegetative propagation

Like many commercial and ornamental plants, orchids can be propagated in a laboratory by various vegetative methods. In fact, orchids were the first ever ornamental plants to be propagated by so-called meristem culture.

### Division

Division is the most usual vegetative method for propagating orchids. Using a spade for this purpose is very much the exception, though this may become necessary with a large specimen of *Cymbidium*.

Sympodial orchids are particularly easy to divide provided there are long enough rhizomes between the pseudobulbs. You

can start preparing several weeks beforehand by cutting the rhizomes and placing a polystyrene chip in each cut to stop it growing back together. The result will be two or more independent plants.

Sometimes individual pseudobulbs (so-called back bulbs) can be used for propagation, but these should be treated as young plants. They contain one or more 'resting eyes' that will sprout with the help of warmth and moisture.

A one-to-one mixture of polystyrene chips with *Sphagnum* or peat is the best substrate for propagation. Warmth (perhaps provided by means of a heating cable) and humidity will enable the shoots to sprout more quickly. Young plants, just like seedlings and meristem cells, require more warmth and shade, and finer substrates, than adult plants.

When dividing plants, always make sure there at least three fully formed pseudobulbs on each plant, as this is essential for flowering.

**Meristem culture**

At one time the most beautiful orchids were also the most expensive. But nowadays, thanks to meristem culture, they have become generally affordable.

Vegetative propagation is important for hybrid orchids because every plant is a one-off. Whereas wild species usually vary only a little, cultivars tend to vary much more. Vegetative propagation ensures the development of identical plants.

Meristem culture involves the use of meristem cells, or plant cells that are capable of dividing and that contain the genetic information for the whole plant. They are placed in a suitable nutritional medium and

*An orchid nursery – meristem culture in a flask*

stimulated into continuous growth. The containers they are grown in are continually being swivelled or shaken. This is to discourage the formation of roots and leaves, keeping them as undifferentiated cells, each of which contains all the genetic information required for growth. When enough cells have formed, the shaking or swivelling is discontinued. Then the roots begin to form under the influence of gravity, as do the leaves on the upper part of the plant.

All the plants developed from one particular culture are genetically identical.

*This Phalaenopsis has formed a keiki ('baby') where a flower would normally have formed. It shouldn't be removed from the parent plant until the roots have formed.*

# What's wrong with my orchid?

Sick orchids are usually caused by faulty treatment. The symptoms aren't always easy to see. The slightest change in the leaves, or more especially the roots, should prompt you to look more closely. Regular checks are essential to make sure you catch any pests or any changes in the plants. The sooner you find any damage, the more effectively you will be able to deal with it.

Damage to roots is often heralded by other tell-tale signs such as algae or moss on the surface of the soil.

The first thing is to distinguish between problems due to faulty treatment and those due to pests and diseases.

- Faulty treatment includes such things as compacted compost, the wrong temperature (either too high or too low), too much (or too little) watering or feeding, or damage from chemicals or pollution.

- Plant diseases may be caused by bacteria, fungi or viruses, whereas other damage may be down to pests such as insects, slugs, mites or small vertebrates.

Most plant damage, with the exception of frost or heat damage, is difficult to spot in time. The symptoms of disease, or of too much or too little feeding, need expert diagnosis.

## Faulty treatment

### Overwatering

As has already been said, overwatering is the commonest cause of problems. If the surface of the soil has become sticky with algae or moss (not the *Sphagnum* that is growing in the substrate, which is a positive sign), this is a symptom of overwatering. Rotting roots and crusty deposits at the root tips are further signs of damage from too much water or salt.

*The heart-shaped leaf on this* Phalaenopsis *is a sure sign that the growing season has begun.*

The best remedy for this is to open up the soil gently with a wooden peg to bring air back to the roots.

Concertina-like growth in the plant itself points to irregular watering – usually too much. The growing shoots keep stopping and starting, and the tissues become deformed to create a concertina-like effect; some shoots may even start to break off.

The solution in this case is to stop watering until the substrate is completely dry, and to repot later on as soon as the new growth becomes apparent, either in the shoots (heart-shaped leaves on *Phalaenopsis*) or in the roots.

When transplanting, you can improve drainage by adding a layer of polystyrene chips (up to a third of the volume of the pot), adding yet more chips to the substrate itself.

### Failure to observe the dormant period correctly

Another very common error is the incorrect observance of the period of dormancy. This leads to symptoms similar to those of water damage.

The growth period, when water, light and nutrients are required, begins with the new

*Concertina-like growth on* Miltonia *and related orchids is a sign of a faulty watering regime that has interfered with the development of the roots.*

shoots – the new roots start even earlier.

This usually happens in the spring, but not always, which is why problems can often occur. With multigeneric hybrids, for example, the new growth starts at intervals of approximately eight months, and this may of course happen in the middle of winter. This means that careful observation is the only way to avoid mistakes.

As soon as new growth begins, you should start watering and feeding your plants, and raise the ambient temperature to about 20°C (68°F), which is about normal room temperature. Extra light may also be necessary in the winter, using one of the daylight lamps that are available from specialist outlets.

*New roots and shoots indicate the start of a new growing season in this sympodial orchid (Catt-leya). Now is the time to repot. But you should take care, because young shoots are very fragile.*

During the weeks that follow, the orchid forms leaves or pseudobulbs depending on the species. They are light green to start with but become darker with time. The leaves develop a leathery surface and the pseudobulbs begin to grow.

It's perfectly possible for a particular orchid to develop pseudobulbs in the spring one

Flowers buds can form before, during or after the dormant period. Flowering is adjusted to the life-cycle of the insects that pollinate the flowers. The stimuli that spark off the flowering process are temperature, dryness and light. Orchids should be fed and watered just so long as the growth season lasts.

year but in the winter the following year. Its water and nutrient requirements will vary depending on the time of year. The plant will naturally grow more during the summer and develop more flowers accordingly.

When the pseudobulb has fully developed, it will be dark green to red in colour, and longer than the spring shoots – now is the point where the dormant season begins. You should water less or even stop watering altogether, depending on the species, and much the same applies to feeding. The end of the dormant period is determined by the plant itself, when it begins to put out new shoots.

## Fungal diseases

- *Pythium* and *Phytophthora* are two fungi that produce brown and black spots, and on *Phalaenopsis* they produce a condition known as heart rot.

- *Rhizoctonia* (root rot) is also common with *Phalaenopsis*, and also with *Cattleya* and *Odontoglossum*. This disease is transmitted by water.

- *Fusarium*, another root fungus, is difficult to diagnose.

*Grey mould* (Botrytis) *has formed on this* Phalaenopsis *flower. This fungus thrives and spreads in cold, damp air, often in the very place where the plant is sold.*

- On the other hand, *Botrytis* – or the familiar grey mould – is a readily recognisable condition. The tiny dark spots are particularly visible on the soft flowers. This fungus thrives in cold and damp conditions, especially in autumn and spring.

## Bacterial diseases

Bacterial infections usually occur as a result of pre-existing fungal disease or pest damage. They are impossible to eradicate completely, even today, and the best policy is to prevent them entirely by taking prompt measures to deal with the fungus or pest.

## Animal pests

Pests are relatively easy to recognise, whether from the little beasts themselves or from the damage they do, and this also makes them much easier to deal with.

Slugs, for example, usually attack at night, but the damage they leave behind is unmistakable. And you may not know exactly what insect is attacking your plant, but you'll certainly know if it's an insect that is involved.

You should always look carefully for any visible changes in your plants such as pale patches, chewed leaves or necrosis (dead tissue). You can often avoid mass infestations by spotting early signs of infestation such as eggs, larvae or pupae.

Ants, for instance, are a frequent precursor of aphids, although this happens more often in a greenhouse than indoors. In the wild, orchids such as *Cattleya* are 'guarded' by ants, which drive the slugs away and are rewarded with the sugar secretions around the buds. But this doesn't apply indoors – you should always get rid of ants from orchids, as they tend to bring aphids with them.

Mice are more of a problem in greenhouses, where they like to feed on the buds and pollen. Setting traps is the best way to combat them.

See the table on pages 42–43 for how to recognise and eradicate various pests such as mites, sciarid flies, aphids, mealy bugs, scale insects, red spider mite, tarsonemid mites, thrips and whitefly.

## Chemical control

Chemical control involves the application of substances that are poisonous to the pests. You should always be careful to apply them exactly according to the manufacturers' instructions, and wear suitable protective clothing (mask and gloves) for the purpose.

- Only use chemicals in rooms you don't normally live in, such as a cellar, a bathroom or a landing.
- If possible, apply the chemicals in the open air, under plastic or in a room you rarely use.
- After you've finished, always make sure that you air the room well.
- Only touch the plants with your gloves on.

*The scale insects on this* Phalaenopsis *need never have got this far. They are much easier to deal with as larvae. Always check for them, taking care to look closely underneath the leaves.*

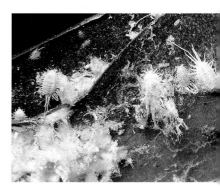

*Mealy bugs protect themselves with a wax-like secretion. They are difficult to combat by chemical means. Biological remedies have proved more successful.*

Protect sensitive buds and flowers from slugs and snails with a collar of dry cotton wool. The creatures find the texture unpleasant. Gravel laid around the pot is similarly effective.

## Biological controls

One biological measure is the application of various herbal preparations to help ward off disease, and which may be sprayed or added to the water (see page 45). But by far the most important form of biological control is the introduction of various native or imported mites, wasps, midges and ladybirds that prey on the different plant pests.

This form of biological warfare carries many advantages. Each predator acts on specific pests, so can be chosen for particular infestations without the danger of side-effects.

These methods are quite simple to use, whether indoors or in a greenhouse or conservatory, the only proviso being that you should follow the accompanying instructions to the letter. You will be able to eradicate not only aphids and red spider mites, but also scale insects, mealy bugs and sciarid flies. Then there is a kind of predatory wasp that kills off the whitefly that plague soft-leaved orchids such as *Calanthe* and *Lycaste*.

These biological controls can be obtained from various specialist mail-order suppliers.

| Problems and how to deal with them | | |
|---|---|---|
| Symptoms | Causes | Remedies |
| **Leaf problems** | | |
| Wilted leaves | Lack of water<br>Overwatering | Increase watering<br>Repot |
| Leaf drop | Dormant phase<br>Overwatering<br>Oxygen deficit<br>Pest infestation | Wait<br>Reduce watering<br>Open up the substrate<br>Diagnose the pest and deal with it |
| Yellow or brown discoloration | Air too dry | Spray, mist or install a humidifier |
| Dried-up leaves | Lack of water<br>Too much fertiliser | Water the plant<br>Rinse out the excess |
| Glassy tissue | Frost damage<br>Bacterial infection | No solution<br>Cut out affected part, fresh air |
| Yellowish-brown spots, sharply defined or glassy | Sunburn<br>Viral infection | Shade<br>Destroy plant |
| Soft, pale-coloured tissue | Not enough light<br><br>Too warm | Improve lighting conditions<br>Reduce temperature |
| Bright leaf colours turn green or yellow | Not enough light | Improve lighting conditions |
| Yellowish-brown leaves, rolled up at the edges | Potassium deficiency (rare) | Potassium-rich fertiliser |
| Leaf veins green, new tissue yellow | Iron deficiency | Iron-rich fertiliser |
| White fuzz with brownish-grey flecks | *Botrytis* (grey mould) | Fresh air, warmth, removal, chemical fungicide |
| Downy or powdery deposit on upper surfaces, rarely on undersides | Mildew | Fresh air, warmth, chemical fungicide |
| Algae and moss | Overwatering | Open up the substrate |
| Small, immovable brown or blackish lumps | Scale insects | Biological control or 'suffocating' spray such as Eradicoat |
| Sticky honeydew, furry black deposit, insects fly up when disturbed | Whitefly<br>Sooty mould | Biological control, insecticidal soap or 'suffocating' spray such as Eradicoat |

| Problems and how to deal with them (contd) | | |
|---|---|---|
| **Symptoms** | **Causes** | **Remedies** |
| **Leaf problems (contd)** | | |
| Light-coloured speckles | Red spider mite – slight infestation | Biological control, insecticidal soap |
| Damaged tissue, silky webbing | – moderate infestation | Biological or chemical control |
| Whole leaf turns yellow | – severe infestation | Remove affected plants |
| Deformed leaves, green, yellowish or black insects, honeydew, sooty mould, attracts ants | Aphids | Biological or chemical control, insecticidal soap |
| Leaves eaten away | Slugs | Slug traps or slug pellets |
| Cork spots, deformities | Tarsonemid mites | Reduce temperature and humidity |
| Silvery tissue, elongated white spots on leaf undersides | Thrips (thunder-flies) and their eggs | Biological or chemical control, sticky traps |
| **Stem problems** | | |
| Long, leggy shoots | Not enough light | Move plant to brighter position |
| Rotting tissue at the base | Bacterial infection | Carefully cut away affected part, then give fresh air |
| **Flower problems** | | |
| Too few buds or buds dropping | Dormant period missed | Observe dormant period |
| | Not enough light | Improve lighting conditions |
| | Over- or under-watering | Reduce or increase watering |
| | Shock from moving plant | Avoid moving plant |
| | Lack of humidity | Humidifier |
| | Pest damage | Find pests and deal with them |
| **Root problems** | | |
| Weak, slimy, brown or thickened roots | Over- or under-watering | Reduce or increase watering |
| | Various possible causes | Ask an expert |

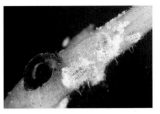

*This Australian ladybird* (Cryptolaemus montrouzieri) *is on a crusade against mealy bugs.*

*A parasitic wasp* called Encarsia formosa *is the best biological remedy for whitefly.*

*Predatory midge larvae* (Aphidolites) *have proved successful against aphids.*

*A predatory mite* (Phytoseiulus persimilis) *is used against the red spider mite.*

Aphids can be successfully removed from hard-leaved plants using a small paintbrush with water and soap. Make sure you collect them all up and destroy them. Aphids can sometimes be removed from orchids simply by spraying them with water.

provide detailed indications. You should always bear in mind that biological controls require more supervision than chemicals, not to mention a certain amount of co-operation from the creatures themselves!

More information on biological controls is available from the suppliers.

**Yellow traps**

These are yet another way to combat pests such as aphids, sciarid flies or even red spider mite. They consist of yellow cards covered with a sticky substance. Insects and mites are attracted to them by the yellow colour and stick fast on contact with the trap.

The number of actual specimens required will depend on how many plants are affected and what stage the infestation has reached. The suppliers

*Odontoglossum 'Violetta' is a long-flowering hybrid descended from O. bictoniense (syn. Lemboglossum bictoniense). Its resemblance to the wild species is very much apparent in this picture.*

| Biological controls available on the market | | | |
|---|---|---|---|
| **Pest** | **Control** | **Where it can be used** | **Conditions for use** |
| Red spider mite | Predatory mite (*Phytoseiulus persimilis*) | Greenhouse, conservatory, windowsill | Temperature above 10°C (50°F), humidity 60–80% |
| Whitefly | Parasitic wasp (*Encarsia formosa*) | Greenhouse, conservatory, windowsill, balcony | Well lit, temperature above 10°C (50°F) |
| Aphids | Predatory midge (*Aphidoletes aphidimyza*) | Greenhouse, conservatory | Above 15°C (59°F); needs at least 12 hours' daylight |
| | Parasitic wasp (*Aphidius matricariae*) | Greenhouse, conservatory | Above 15°C (59°F); only possible from November to June |
| Thrips (thunderflies) | Predatory mite (*Ambliseius cucumeris*) | Greenhouse, conservatory | High humidity, warm – i.e. above 16°C (61°F) |
| Mealy bugs | Australian ladybird (*Cryptolaemus montrouzieri*) | Greenhouse, conservatory, windowsill | Above 20°C (68°F), high humidity |
| Sciarid fly larvae | Predatory mite (*Hypoaspis miles*) | Greenhouse, conservatory, patio, windowsill, balcony | Substrate temperature above 12°C (54°F) |

## Gentle measures

Where orchids have already been damaged, only limited treatment is possible. So it is best to prevent diseases or pests before they attack. One method is to use one of the herbal brews below. If they smell unpleasant, the stench can be reduced by adding valerian extract.

### Stinging nettle/comfrey brew

- Improves the plant's natural resistance (comfrey especially).
- Place 200 g of dried herbs or 1 kg of fresh herbs (collect stinging nettles when in flower) in 10 litres of water and allow it to ferment for 1–2 weeks. Add 10 litres of water for every litre of the brew. Spray once every fortnight.

### Field horsetail extract

- Strengthens plant tissues.
- Guards against fungal infection.
- Soak 200 g of dried herbs or 1 kg of fresh herbs for 24 hours in 10 litres of cold water. Add 10 litres of water for every 2 litres of the brew. Water or spray the plant.

### Tansy extract

- Repels insects and mites.
- Soak 30 g of dried herbs or 500 g of fresh herbs for 24 hours in 10 litres of cold water. Dilute with 20 litres of water and spray over your plants.

### Onion and garlic tea

- Improves resistance to fungal disease.
- Pour boiling water over 80 g of chopped onion/garlic cloves and allow to infuse for 3 hours. Strain the liquid and dilute with 10 litres of water. Spray every 10–14 days.

## *at a glance*

**Why aren't my orchids flowering?**

- Too warm or not warm enough.
- Dormant period not observed.
- Plants weakened by the wrong treatment or infestation by pests such as mites or thrips.

**How much light do orchids need?**

- As much as possible but avoid burning.
- Some orchids require shade for a few weeks a year.
- With some orchids, on the other hand, supplementary lighting may be required.

**How often should they be watered?**

- Depends on the stage of growth.
- Only when the plants have properly dried out.
- Never water orchids simply as a precaution!

**How often do they need feeding, and what with?**

- You will find a number of fertilisers available, but those formulated for orchids should be adequate.
- The nutrient balance is important. It should normally be NPK 1:1:1, though more nitrogen is needed at the beginning of the growing season or with bark substrates.
- There is little significant difference between mineral and organic fertilisers. However, organic feeds work more slowly, and should only be given if the roots are healthy.
- Feed once for every three times you water.

**Are orchids susceptible to a lot of diseases?**

- No more and no less than any other houseplant.
- There are no specific orchid diseases.

# Orchids as houseplants

Nowadays orchids have become extremely popular as houseplants. Other exciting possibilities include orchid cases and displays in a greenhouse or conservatory.

## Orchids on a windowsill

Orchids are undoubtedly among the most rewarding of houseplants. The moth orchid (*Phalaenopsis*) probably flowers for longer than any other houseplant, and also requires less care than most other plants.

### Orchids are typical houseplants

It can generally be said that orchids will flourish in the same places where other tropical plants bloom and grow. If a *Hibiscus*, an African violet or a Christmas cactus will flower, then so will a *Phalaenopsis*, a *Cattleya* or a × *Vuylstekeara* Cambria.

*◄ Miniature* Cymbidium *hybrids make up for their small flowers with a luxuriant profusion of blooms. The plants themselves, which can scarcely be described as miniature, are more heat-tolerant than the large-flowered varieties of* Cymbidium.

To create tropical conditions indoors, you may need a window trough (see page 28), a humidifier or a mister, or regular spraying may suffice. A shortage of light – at a north-facing window, for example – can be rectified using a daylight lamp. Given the choice, a southerly aspect is preferable, though some shade will be needed from April onwards. Often a curtain or venetian blinds will be enough.

Choosing the right location is a more difficult task, and depends very much on the function of each room in the house. A living room won't be right for a dormant plant requiring 10°C (50°F), for example, while a bedroom is seldom heated to 20°C (68°F). If you want a particular orchid – a *Phalaenopsis*, say – but only have a cool room available, then you could invest in a heated mat or tray to raise the temperature of the roots. This should enable even tropical plants to survive in a cooler room.

*Window displays like this one hark back to the days of the 19th century. They are only rarely seen nowadays, which is a shame given all that can be achieved with modern science and technology.*

*Coelogyne cristata was a popular orchid in our grandparents' generation. It should be kept frost-free in winter, but prefers the open air during the summer.*

*A typical community of epiphytic plants on a tree in South America, with bromeliads, ferns and orchids. This provides the model for an epiphytic plant community on a mount in the home.*

Orchids that thrive in temperate zones should do very well in the garden during the summer. They require half-shade and protection from prolonged rain and pests such as slugs.

The dormant period also has to be provided for, either by keeping the plant drier or by moving it to a cooler room. Even a mount, a bowl or a basket can be moved to a windowsill, where they look very decorative.

There should be a big enough range of orchids available for you to be able to find plants that are suited to particular rooms in the house:

- **warm greenhouse orchids** for the living room
- **temperate greenhouse orchids** for the bedroom
- **cold greenhouse orchids** for an unheated room that remains frost-free.

## An epiphytic community on a mount

A mount is the most natural way of growing orchids; although difficult, this can even be achieved indoors. The best model for a mount is the epiphytic community where orchids grow in the wild in the company of plants such as bromeliads, ferns, *Philodendron*, *Ficus repens* or *Peperomia*.

Only healthy trunks or branches should be used as mounts. Gnarled vines are also very decorative, and can be tied together to make a 'tree'. A mount must be able to last for at least eight years. An alternative method is to use plastic tubing covered with cork bark.

The mount has to be thoroughly cleaned before you start. A wire brush, or hot water from a high-pressure sprayer, should be enough to remove any unwanted pests from the bark. A really firm base is also essential – a concrete footing, for example – to hold the weight of the growing community of plants. It may also be necessary to secure the mount to a window, a wall or a ceiling with wires or chains. A container will also be needed at the base for some of the companion plants.

The companion plants should be installed first. One of the best base plants is the creeping fig (*Ficus pumila*), which winds

*Great care is needed when attaching a mount to its base, as it should be neither too tight nor too loose.*

*A mounted display in a living room. A shallow bowl filled with moist clay pellets helps to raise the humidity, and the mount has been fixed to the wall for stability.*

itself quickly around the branch. Other companion plants may be used according to taste, and depending on the lighting conditions. Bromeliads with leaf rosettes should be tied to the mount in such a way that the rosettes stay upright and can hold water. Only when the companion plants have become established should the orchids be added to the community.

While a lot of spraying will still be needed, the companion plants will help to maintain the humidity levels thanks to the moisture released from their leaves.

## An orchid case

Ever since orchids were first brought back from South America to Britain in Wardian cases, people have endeavoured to create small protected biotopes for these sensitive plants. Yet only recently has it become possible to realise this dream properly. Modern technology has now enabled us to overcome the many associated problems of overheating, waterlogging and shortage of light, air and humidity. A lot has been achieved using the example of the aquarium.

To fix epiphytes to a mount, use only a little substrate, followed by a little *Sphagnum*, and tie the plant firmly using copper wire, nylon thread or old tights. Take great care not to damage the roots. The substrate will shrink as it dries out, so after a week some tightening will be needed.

*An orchid case containing a mounted display. This glass case is ideal for creating an epiphytic community in a stable humid environment. Some extra lighting is recommended.*

There are very few ready-made orchid cases on the market, and all of them are expensive. This leaves the option of DIY or working with a manufacturer to create your own orchid case. A terrarium (see below) provides a good design model.

It's important to include following features:

- small vents at the top and bottom of the glass case
- large glass doors to provide access when necessary
- some ventilation to keep the air circulating
- lighting – installed outside the case to avoid problems of overheating.

The case may be made purely of glass, or it may have a wooden, steel or aluminium frame. The choice is a matter of taste but will also depend on your budget. It may be possible to line the back of the case with cork bark on which plants can be mounted.

The choice of plants for an orchid case is still influenced by its surroundings. It's possible to provide extra heat, but not to reduce the temperature inside the case.

Some heating may need to be installed, depending on the anticipated temperature outside the case. Heated mats or cables need thermostatic controls, and in view of the high humidity inside, all electrical installations should be properly insulated. If a mount is to be included, this should be firmly fixed.

The substrate in the bottom of the case should be firmly structured. A mixture of orchid compost with clay pellets or Seramis has proved very good.

## Orchids in a terrarium

A terrarium is a kind of display case too. However, the choice of plants may be more limited as the climatic conditions inside will be to a certain extent determined by the animals to be kept in the terrarium. Orchids with their sturdy leaves and roots should make ideal candidates, but it's important to create the right **plant community**. What animals will you be keeping? What will their diet be? And how large or heavy will they be?

The technical considerations are similar to those for orchid cases (see above). Once the case has been built, you should first install a community of

**companion plants**. These might include a creeping fig (*Ficus pumila*), which comes in a special dwarf variety called *F. pumila* 'Minima'. Other good candidates are *Episcia, Acorus, Fittonia, Spathiphyllum* and green bromeliads. *Tillandsia* is only suitable for a cooler terrarium that is particularly brightly lit. Ferns on the floor of the terrarium are easy to look after, as are epiphytes such as *Selaginella* or *Peperomia*.

All new specimens should first be kept in quarantine and regularly checked. Woodlice and slugs, which can so easily be brought in with the plants, can be searched for in the dark with the help of a torch.

Any live food for the animals in the terrarium will include plant-eaters, so it should be given in small measured quantities so that it won't survive to do any damage.

While everyday care is not too difficult, dealing with pests can be problematic. All poisons are ruled out, while biological controls may be limited in effect, as they may easily do no more than provide extra food for the animals. So it's absolutely essential to make sure that any plants you introduce are completely free of pests.

## A paludarium

A paludarium is a combination of an aquarium and a terrarium, and may include both plants and animals, land and water. The size will depend on what you want to put in it.

*A paludarium contains a ready-made solution to the problem of humidity. Lighting conditions can be adjusted by the positioning of plant lamps.*

Once the green plants have been installed in a terrarium, then the orchids can follow and finally the animals. The right orchids to choose will depend on the temperature and on the size of the orchids, which should be limited to genera and species that don't go through a marked dormant phase.

Weight can often be a problem on account of the aquarium section of the paludarium. The usual pattern is to have one-third aquarium to two-thirds terrarium.

The overall height including the base will be limited by the height of the ceiling. The base will need to accommodate all the electrical system, including the water filter, the wiring etc.

The water will provide plenty of humidity to support plants from wet tropical or subtropical regions. It is possible to program the lighting so that day and night are each 12 hours long throughout the year, and the temperature can be kept at a constant 24°C (75°F).

The plants can range from water plants to swamp vegetation and epiphytes. The top part of the paludarium, especially around the lights, can be reserved for plants needing a drier atmosphere.

The plants must again be fully established before any animals are introduced. And the land animals need to be chosen with great care – plant-eaters such as the ever-popular terrapins are effectively ruled out.

It's not easy to create a self-contained system in which water and nutrients are recycled and the correct temperature and humidity are maintained. There are no foolproof recipes or solutions, and there is a tremendous amount of work involved checking the animals and plants, and intervening where necessary. And above all, patience will be needed in order to succeed.

Water gardens built with tiles, baths and felt are OK for professional gardeners, but less suitable for amateurs and even less so for orchids. Orchids with 'wet feet' are liable to fungal disease.

# Greenhouse orchids

For many orchid growers, a greenhouse will remain nothing more than just a dream, whether for reasons of cost, lack of time or simply lack of space. And alas, for those who do finally get their greenhouse, the results can so easily become a nightmare. After years of success with orchids on a windowsill, a greenhouse can be a recipe for failure. A small greenhouse may provide optimum conditions for growing orchids, but it also provides an ideal haunt for pests, and mistakes are so easily made.

Not every greenhouse on the market is suitable for growing orchids, although any kind of greenhouse can be used on a temporary basis in the summer. An orchid greenhouse must be well insulated, with double glazing and firm, frost-free foundations. Here are some further suggestions on the basis of experience:

- The greenhouse should be placed in a sheltered position along an east–west axis.
- It doesn't matter whether the frame is made of aluminium, steel or wood, although aluminium bars, which for structural reasons are built

with slit openings, provide the means for attaching hanging baskets, trellises etc.

- At least 20% of the glass should be capable of being opened for ventilation (doors and windows).
- Some form of shade is needed for orchids either inside or outside the greenhouse. Movable blinds are the best solution, although they take more trouble to install.
- Heating elements should not produce a lot of surface heat as this dries out the air. Hot-water pipes are therefore the best solution.
- Electrical fan heaters should be run on their slowest setting.

Perhaps the best form of shade is provided by plants. This also has the added advantage of providing extra humidity.

The best candidates for this include a greenhouse vine (e.g. a grapevine), passion flower (*Passiflora edulis, P. caerulea* or *P. quadrangularis*), birthwort (*Aristolochia littoralis*), creeping fig (*Ficus pumila*) and *Philodendron*. Some of them retain their foliage in winter, which can deprive the orchids of light. Heavy pruning once a year is therefore essential.

The floor of the greenhouse should not be sealed with concrete. Only the footways need to be of a hard material.

The best position for care and maintenance is to have the pots on benches lined with metal or wooden lattices (using untreated wood, of course). Shelves or hanging benches provide yet more possibilities. The benches should be at least 90 cm (3 ft) off the floor, or else it won't be possible to look at the plants properly.

## Choice of plants and plant conservation

Given the high humidity levels in a greenhouse, it is possible to mount orchids on branches of cork oak, grapevine or hardwood. The best tying materials for this purpose are nylon thread or tights.

The sun heats up the air in a greenhouse very much faster than in the house or in the open air. High humidity is the only way to prevent the plants from overheating.

If you're planning on having orchids in a new greenhouse, then it's worth bearing in mind that they can be looked after more effectively in combination with other plants. So don't

*A conservatory provides the ideal conditions for orchids, because it's easier to achieve the necessary humidity levels than inside the house.*

leave the greenhouse half empty. A few orchids can always be supplemented by a variety of large-leaved plants (including annuals) or even vegetables. The transpiration from all the plants will help create the humidity levels that the plant community requires.

Old-fashioned **stove houses** are also good for orchids. While the lighting is not so good, the humidity and temperature are easier to control, and the heating bills will be lower.

Greenhouses can be classified as cold, temperate or warm depending on the temperature (see the table on page 17). Your choice of plants will be determined by which type of greenhouse you have created.

Greenhouse plants are vulnerable to more pests, including mealy bugs, scale insects and especially snails. In winter even mice will come in search of pollen.

Fungal or bacterial diseases may be the result of too much or too little heat. The best way to avoid them is to get the temperature right, keep the air circulating, and above all provide plenty of fresh air.

*Orchids in a greenhouse. A ventilator helps the air to circulate, while a special greenhouse lamp provides extra light for young or budding plants.*

## Orchids in a conservatory

From a practical point of view a conservatory is no more than a better insulated greenhouse. The requirements are therefore similar but not identical.

There are effectively two kinds of conservatory. The first is modelled on the classic winter garden, where Mediterranean tub plants are grown along with palms and orchids that need to be kept cool.

The second type of conservatory is more usual these days, namely a glass-covered extension to the house that combines similar temperatures to those indoors with better lighting conditions.

The orchids you choose for the latter should be of the sort that grow in warmer climes such as *Phalaenopsis* and some *Paphiopedilum* or *Dendrobium* species. The care requirements are similar to those for indoor orchids (see pages 47 ff.), except that more shade is normally required unless your conservatory has a northerly aspect.

One very good way to produce the humidity required for warm greenhouse orchids is to create small plant communities with plenty of large-leaved plants that give off moisture. You might, for example, prefer bromeliads on a mount, with water collecting in their leaf rosettes, or maybe climbing plants such as *Philodendron* or *Allamanda*. Hanging baskets planted with *Columnea*, *Platycerium* or leaf cacti are another good choice.

Other helpful features might include a small fountain or

some other kind of water feature, or a plant trough with clay pellets in the bottom.

## Orchids hate air conditioning

Conservatories with air conditioning are intended primarily for human comfort, whereas plants, including orchids, are adversely affected by air conditioning, because for them draughts may prove fatal. Moreover, such conservatories often lack the necessary roof ventilation that may sometimes be required for short periods, even in winter.

A cool conservatory of the sort that is used for Mediterranean tub plants, and that we may occupy in the summer or on sunny days in winter, is better suited to orchids requiring more temperate conditions. Like the tub plants, they can be moved out into the garden during the summer. The humidity is normally sufficient, thanks to the presence of other plants and the cooler temperatures. And for plants in their dormant phase the humidity may in fact be dangerously high.

Depending on the exact temperature conditions, the best plants for a cool conserva-tory, apart from citrus plants, are *Cymbidium, Rossio-glossum,* × *Odontioda* and some *Laelia* species, as well as fuchsias and chrysanthemums. As always, the right choice will vary. Among the most popular choices are the winter-flowering orchids – early-flowering *Cymbidium,* the well-known *Coelogyne cristata, Laelia autumnalis* and others.

Even earlier than in the garden outside, spring warmth is followed by the arrival of aphids on the hunt for new shoots to feast on. Ants assist them in this process, enabling them to spread more quickly. The buds and flowers of the winter-flowering orchids are among the most frequent victims. The only way to contain them is careful observation followed by the installation of sticky yellow traps, biological controls and various organic preparations.

Never move plants with a lot of buds (e.g. *Camellia* or *Cymbidium*) during the winter. Leave them where they are until flowering has finished and they can be moved. Winter buds can be protected from snails using cotton wool (see page 41).

When the humidity is reduced, keep an even keener eye out for red spider mite. A conservatory is the ideal place for biological controls. The introduction of predatory mites has proved one of the most effective ways of eradicating red spider mite.

## *at a glance*

- Raise the humidity in the room by using a window trough and if possible by placing orchids in plant communities together with other plants.

- Epiphyte mounts need to be firmly fixed in place, but the plants shouldn't be tied on too tightly.

- Make sure an orchid case is sufficiently ventilated, using a fan for extra ventilation.

- In a terrarium or a paludarium, the plants should be installed first before animals are introduced.

- A conservatory should be well ventilated, but not by means of air conditioning as this is bad for plants.

- The choice of orchids depends on the temperatures that prevail in whatever place they are planted.

# The most beautiful orchids

We can't list all the most beautiful orchids, because there are so many of them and the choice is a matter of personal taste, but the selection we have made here should provide a good taster.

## Breeding and hybridisation

The fostering of particular characteristics is vital to the survival of all living things. But significant changes usually take many generations to develop. Genetic variations that occur spontaneously as a result of changes in chromosomes are known as mutations. The aim of breeding is to influence the genes of a plant so as to foster particular characteristics such as the size or durability of the flowers.

Plants in the wild ensure the furtherance of their species by adapting themselves to just one pollinator (usually an insect in the case of orchids). But when humans take over the task of pollination, they can transcend not only geographical boundaries but also those determined by pollination. This allows for

*◀ × Doritaenopsis hybrids are the result of crossing the two genera Doritis and Phalaenopsis. Their flowers are longer-lasting and more brightly coloured than those of either parent genus, and the plants will tolerate more light and cooler temperatures.*

the creation of completely new hybrids that couldn't possibly have existed in the wild.

After pollination, the pollen grains develop small appendages that penetrate the ovary of the plant, where the male and female cells become fused. Orchids are unusual, however, in that each female cell in the ovary is fertilised by a separate pollen grain. This means that the offspring of a single pollination will vary among themselves, albeit within certain limits.

Orchids have yet another characteristic that gives them the edge over other houseplants. This is the fact that you can cross orchids not only within the species (which is normally the case anyway) and with other species in the genus, but also with other genera.

### Breeding success

Orchid breeding began in Britain in 1856, since which time more than 60,000 orchid hybrids have been created, and that only includes those which have been officially registered.

All new breeds of orchids throughout the world, if they are to be officially recognised, have to be registered in Britain, where they are recorded in *Sander's List of Orchid Hybrids*.

It's possible to trace the 'genealogy' of a particular strain from the name alone. The familiar Cambria orchids, for example, are officially called × *Vuylstekeara* Cambria. This particular group of hybrids, created in 1931, illustrates how complicated the relationships between intergeneric hybrids had already become. Some genealogies have now become virtually impossible to trace.

Knowledge of such details can be a very useful guide to the correct care of a particular hybrid, provided there are not too many genera involved and all the parent species originated in the same region, as is the case with our example above. Most of the parent species of the × *Vuylstekeara* Cambria hybrids grow in cool regions,

Orchid breeding is even possible for amateurs. All you have to do is to buy the necessary equipment, and you can create your own orchid hybrid in your kitchen.

Cochlioda noezliana, *an ancestor of* × Vuylstekeara *Cambria, comes from Peru. Its flowers are always popular.*

× Vuylstekeara *Cambria 'Plush' FCC/RHS was produced in 1931 – one of many hybrids created from the three genera* Miltoniopsis, Cochlioda *and* Odontoglossum. *The name Cambria is used as a collective term for a whole group of orchid hybrids.*

growers, who are now being joined by an expanding number of amateurs, choose new strains on the basis of specific external features such as colour, shape,

so most Cambrias will similarly like cooler conditions. The genus × *Vuylstekeara* originated from the three genera *Cochlioda*, *Miltonia* (*Miltoniopsis*) and *Odontoglossum*. The hybrid genus was named after the Belgian orchid breeder Charles Vuylsteke. The multiplication sign (×) indicates a hybrid genus, while the ending -*ara* shows that we are dealing with multigeneric hybrids.

### New houseplants

Intergeneric hybrids allow us to develop totally new houseplants or cut flowers. Professional

Miltoniopsis vexillaria *is a parent species of most modern breeds of pansy orchid* (Miltoniopsis/Miltonia), *and also of hybrids such as* × Vuylstekeara *Cambria.*

Odontoglossum crispum *is probably the most important parent species of* × Vuylstekeara. *It is still one of our most delightful orchids.*

durability and size. Intuition and chance also play an important part. Moreover, professionals have taken advantage of insights gained from the breeding of other plants, using chemicals or radiation to influence their genetic structure – though success has been limited so far.

Not every hybrid is a success. Over 100 attempts may be needed before a new strain is achieved. Even when a seed has formed, there's no guarantee it will germinate, or that the new plant will grow properly. The time required from the creation of a new strain of *Paphiopedilum* to the final flowering can be as long as eight years. This is no hobby for the impatient!

### Outstanding orchid breeds

Special honours aren't just confined to people. Plants too may be honoured on the basis of outstanding achievement. All new strains of orchid are registered in Britain, but many of them are also presented to a committee for assessment. Those breeds that are deemed to be of outstanding quality are given a special title after their names, after the fashion of the Queen's Birthday Honours. The highest honour to be bestowed is the First Class Certificate

(FCC). One orchid to be so honoured was *Odontoglossum crispum* var. *pacho* FCC/RHS, where RHS stands for the awarding body, the Royal Horticultural Society. There are of course other awards available.

In the meantime, other countries such as Germany, Japan and the USA have introduced their own awards modelled on the British system.

## Protecting endangered species

Endangered orchids aren't confined to Britain. Many tropical orchids are similarly faced with extinction. By the early 19th century, some species had already fallen victim to the greed of collectors. Today the destruction of the tropical rainforests, combined with efforts of some collectors to obtain rare and forbidden plants, has sealed the fate of many species. Many orchids will never even be known about because they will have been destroyed before they could even be discovered.

The Washington Convention on International Trade in Endangered Species of Wild Fauna and Flora (CITES) came into force in 1975, and so far 115 states have signed up to it.

Cypripedium calceolus, *our native lady's slipper orchid, is a protected species. Like the tropical slipper orchids,* Paphiopedilum *and* Phragmipedium, *it has a lip that is shaped like a slipper.*

All orchid species listed in its appendix are considered to be in need of protection. Some are

When buying orchids at a market or exhibition, always ask the salesperson for a CITES certificate (i.e. from the Convention on International Trade in Endangered Species). This will indicate that the statutory requirements have been fulfilled, and that the plant has been obtained from breeding stock and not from the wild.

× Wilsonara *'Kolibri' shows a definite resemblance to* Oncidium, *which is one of its parent genera. Its branching sprays of flowers will last for weeks.*

Make sure you have the full botanical name of any plant you wish to buy. Sometimes this will be clear from only part of the name – Cambria 'Orange', for example. If you're only interested in a particular plant, then it's a good idea to know exactly what you're looking for.

excluded from sale altogether, while others may only be sold by those in possession of a specific permit. The details of the agreement are regulated by individual states.

If you're thinking of bringing an orchid back from a holiday abroad as a souvenir, remember that wild orchids are banned. You may, however, be able to bring an artificially propagated plant into the country provided it has a permit and meets phytosanitary regulations. If in doubt, check first with the Department for Environment, Food and Rural Affairs.

Don't worry about buying an orchid at your local garden centre or florist – they will almost certainly have ensured that the regulations have been complied with.

## Botanical names

The enormous variety of plants, and the fact that they know no boundaries of language or culture, meant that an international method of nomenclature was necessary in order to classify them accurately. The binary nomenclature that we now have was introduced by the Swedish botanist Carl von Linné in 1758. According to this system all plants (and animals) are subdivided into families, genera and species. The way the names are written down is also regulated, and international bodies have been appointed to check that the regulations are followed.

A good example is the botanical name for the clown orchid (see page 20), which was originally given as *Odontoglossum grande*. Nowadays the correct name for this species is *Rossioglossum grande*. Name changes such as this one are not arbitrary – they must be properly justified, and are usually based on new botanical evidence.

The species *Miltoniopsis roezlii* has already been mentioned on page 7. The genus *Miltonia* (pansy orchids) was established in 1837 and named after Viscount Milton, later Earl Fitzwilliam (1786–1857), of Wentworth House in Yorkshire, a great horticultural patron and owner of an orchid collection. In 1889 the genus was divided into two genera – *Miltonia* and *Miltoniopsis* (meaning 'resembling *Miltonia*') – on botanical grounds, because some pansy orchids showed small differences in the structure of the flower and pseudobulbs. However, this division was never officially recognised, and in

1976 botanists reunited the genus under the name *Miltoniopsis*. If you buy from a specialist nursery, you will probably find that *Miltonia* is used for species from Brazil, while those from Panama, Colombia and Ecuador are called *Miltoniopsis*. However, you may still find both kinds sold as *Miltonia* in some shops and nurseries.

### The correct nomenclature

The botanical name begins with the **genus** (generic name), which is given in italics with an initial capital – *Miltoniopsis*, for example. This is followed by the **species** (specific name), which is again in italics but without an initial capital – *Miltoniopsis roezlii*. If the plant is a **variety**, the name of the variety follows that of the species thus: **var.** *alba* (white) or **var.** *grandiflora* (large-flowered).

In the case of a **hybrid**, the generic name is retained and is immediately followed by the hybrid group, which is given with initial capitals but not in italics – *Miltoniopsis* **Maiers Liebling**, for example. If a particular hybrid within the group is to be given, then the name of the hybrid, also known as the **cultivar** (cultivated variety), is

added, again with initial capitals but also with inverted commas: *Miltoniopsis* **Maiers Liebling 'Rotes Licht'**.

Where species from two different genera are crossed, this creates an **intergeneric hybrid** with a generic name that combines the names of both parent genera, while a multiplication sign (✕) is used to indicate a cross or hybrid. The combination *Cattleya* ✕ *Sophronites* (a frequent cross) gives the generic name ✕ *Sophrocattleya*, which is followed by the hybrid group and/or cultivar name.

Where three or more genera are involved, the resulting **multigeneric hybrid** is given a more fanciful name, usually combining the name of the person who bred the first such hybrid (e.g. Vuylsteke) with the ending *–ara* to indicate that it derives from at least three genera – ✕ *Vuylstekeara*. Thus the name of the cultivar ✕ *Vuylstekeara* Cambria 'Orange' is made up of the genus: ✕ *Vuylstekeara*; the hybrid group: Cambria; and the cultivar (cv): 'Orange'.

The number of orchid hybrids has risen over the years to more than 60,000, to which 1,500 are added each year – an unbelievable number!

# Intergeneric hybrids

The table overleaf gives the generic names of a selection of intergeneric and multigeneric hybrids, indicating the genera from which they are descended. The internationally agreed abbreviations are given in brackets. If you buy a plant from any of these genera, knowledge of the parent genera will provide useful initial information about how to look after it. (There is a similar table on page 85.)

✕ Odontocidium *'Susan Kaufman' is a cultivar deriving from* Oncidium flexuosum. *It grows fast and produces a beautiful and long-lasting display of small flowers.*

## The most important hybrid genera

| Hybrid genera | Produced from the following genera |
|---|---|
| × *Ascocenda* (*Ascda*) | *Ascocentrum* (*Asctm*) × *Vanda* (*V.*) |
| × *Balaguerara* (*Blga*) | *Broughtonia* (*Bro.*) × *Epidendrum* (*Epi.*) × *Laeliopsis* (*Lps.*) × *Tetramicra* (*Ttma*) |
| × *Brassocattleya* (Bc.) | *Brassavola* (*B.*) × *Cattleya* (*C.*) |
| × *Brassolaelia* (Bl.) | *Brassavola* (*B.*) × *Laelia* (*L.*) |
| × *Brassolaeliocattleya* (Blc.) | *Brassavola* (*B.*) × *Cattleya* (*C.*) × *Laelia* (*L.*) |
| × *Burrageara* (*Burr.*) | *Cochlioda* (*Cda*) × *Miltonia* (*Milt.*) × *Odontoglossum* (*Odm*) × *Oncidium* (*Onc.*) |
| × *Doritaenopsis* (*Dtps*) | *Doritis* (*Dor.*) × *Phalaenopsis* (*Phal.*) |
| × *Epicattleya* (*Epc.*) | *Cattleya* (*C.*) × *Epidendrum* (*Epi.*) |
| × *Goodaleara* (*Gdlra*) | *Brassia* (*Brs.*) × *Cochlioda* (*Cda*) × *Miltonia* (Milt.) × *Odontoglossum* (*Odm*) × *Oncidium* (*Onc.*) |
| × *Maclellanara* (*Mclna*) | *Brassia* (*Brs.*) × *Odontoglossum* (*Odm*) × *Oncidium* (*Onc.*) |
| × *Miltonidium* (*Mtdm*) | *Miltonia* (*Milt.*) × *Oncidium* (*Onc.*) |
| × *Mooreara* (*Mora*) | *Brassavola* (*B.*) × *Broughtonia* (*Bro.*) × *Cattleya* (*C.*) × *Laelia* (*L.*) × *Schomburgkia* (*Schom.*) × *Sophronitis* (*Soph.*) |
| × *Odontioda* (*Oda*) | *Cochlioda* (*Cda*) × *Odontoglossum* (*Odm*) |
| × *Odontobrassia* (*Odbrs.*) | *Brassia* (*Brs.*) × *Odontoglossum* (*Odm*) |
| × *Odontocidium* (*Odcdm*) | *Odontoglossum* (*Odm*) × *Oncidium* (*Onc.*) |
| × *Odontonia* (*Odtna*) | *Miltonia* (*Milt.*) × *Odontoglossum* (*Odm.*) |
| × *Sophrocattleya* (*Sc.*) | *Cattleya* (*C.*) × *Sophronitis* (*Soph.*) |
| × *Sophrolaeliocattleya* (*Slc.*) | *Cattleya* (*C.*) × *Laelia* (*L.*) × *Sophronitis* (*Soph.*) |
| × *Vuylstekeara* (*Vuyl.*) | *Cochlioda* (*Cda*) × *Miltonia* (*Milt.*) × *Odontoglossum* (*Odm*) |
| × *Westara* (*Wsta*) | *Brassavola* (*B.*) × *Broughtonia* (*Bro.*) × *Cattleya* (*C.*) × *Laelia* (*L.*) × *Schomburgkia* (*Schom.*) |
| × *Wilsonara* (*Wils.*) | *Cochlioda* (*Cda*) × *Odontoglossum* (*Odm*) × *Oncidium* (*Onc.*) |

# The best orchid genera

### *Phalaenopsis*
### Moth orchids

If there is one orchid genus that deserves to be called a house-plant, then it is *Phalaenopsis*. This is scarcely surprising given that in the Philippines, where the most important species, *P. amabilis*, originates, the climate is always warm, as in our modern centrally-heated houses. Other *Phalaenopsis* species come from Myanmar (Burma), southern China and Queensland in Australia.

There are large numbers of hybrids, thanks partly to the fact that the time from seeding to final flowering is relatively short (three years), though a further eight months is required for the seeds to ripen.

Both white and pink varieties retain their purity fairly well when propagated by seed. However, meristem (plant tissue) culture is commonly used to preserve particular colours and shapes of flowers.

Intergeneric hybrids such as those with *Ascocentrum* and *Renanthera* are of interest but have yet to become established.

Only hybrids with *Doritis*, known as × *Doritaenopsis*, have proved successful so far. These hybrids grow more slowly and the flower takes longer to develop. On the other hand, the flowers are longer-lasting and have particularly bright colours.

Apart from the cultivars, the following species are available:

• **P. amabilis** has 50-cm (20-in) leaves and a branching, more-or-less overhanging flower stem up to 1 m (40 in) tall. Individual flowers measure 8 cm (3 in) across,

Phalaenopsis *'Carmela's Pixie' is just what an indoor orchid should be – lots of flowers on a beautifully proportioned stem, and easy to look after.*

and are white with a yellow base to the lip. Origins: Australia, Philippines, Indonesia.

• **P. schilleriana** has 45-cm (17-in) leaves and a similar flower stem to *P. amabilis*. Large specimens may have as many as 200 flowers. Individual flowers measure 7 cm (3 in) across, and are softly or intensely pink with red speckles on the sides of the lip. Origins: Philippines. The most important of the pink species after *P. sanderiana*, *P. schilleriana* requires a day–night temperature difference of at least 5C° (9F°) to be sure of flowering.

• **P. stuartiana** is similar to *P. schilleriana* in terms of its origins, culture and appearance, except that the flowers are white, speckled with brownish red.

• **P. equestris** is small but extremely pretty, with 20-cm (8-in) leaves and a 40-cm (16-in) flower stem. Individual flowers measure up to

Phalaenopsis schilleriana *was named after the Hamburg merchant in whose house it first flowered in 1860.*

4 cm (1.5 in) across; pink to magenta in colour. Origins: Taiwan, Philippines. Popular pot plant, requiring less water and more light-tolerant than other species.

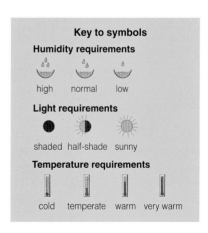

**Key to symbols**

**Humidity requirements**

high    normal    low

**Light requirements**

shaded   half-shade   sunny

**Temperature requirements**

cold   temperate   warm   very warm

Phalaenopsis stuartiana *doesn't flower for as long as* P. amabilis, *but on the other hand it can flower in any season. The flowers grow mostly on branching sprays.*

- **P. amboinensis** is a similarly attractive orchid, with fleshy leaves that are about 30 cm (12 in) long. The flower stem is 35 cm (14 in) long and only carries a few blooms.

If it is looked after well, a *Phalaenopsis* will flower as often as two or three times a year. After the first flowering, prune the flower stem down to the last two or three nodes, cutting just above a node. The plant will flower again after about 120 days, and may perhaps even flower a third time.

Individual flowers are 6 cm (2.5 in) across, and brownish yellow to yellow, with diagonal brown or reddish-brown stripes. This species may flower almost all year round. Origins: Moluccas, Ambon, Celebes.

### Cultivars

*Phalaenopsis* orchids are bred for their compact, many-branched sprays of flowers. There is a preference for varieties that flower again after the old flower stem has been pruned. The choice of moth orchids is extremely wide, with

Phalaenopsis lueddemanniana *is a very variable species. The plant develops lots of keikis, which can be left on the plant so that it becomes large and bushy.*

Phalaenopsis *'Woodlawn' is an old cultivar from the United States. The large flowers last for many weeks. Similar varieties on the market include* P. *'Flare Spots' and* P. *'Follett'.*

something to cater for every taste – pure white, dark lilac, yellow, speckled, striped.

### General advice

*Phalaenopsis* shouldn't be kept in too much shade, as this slows down growth and reduces flowering.

- **Temperature:** minimum 17°C (63°F) by day, 16°C (61°F) by night; ideal temperature 22°C (72°F) by day, lower by night.

- **Light:** moderate requirements, though supplementary lighting is desirable in winter. The buds are in fact sensitive to poor light or low temperatures, which may sometimes cause them to drop in autumn or winter. Unfortunately here is no way of preventing this.

- **Repotting:** at least once every two years.

- **Pests and diseases:** check plants for mealy bugs and scale insects. *Phalaenopsis* is liable to *Botrytis* if it is kept in a greenhouse or conservatory, though not indoors. New shoots are particularly sensitive, so water should never be allowed to collect around them.

- **Special features:** some species and varieties produce keikis (see picture on page 38). This often happens in response to poor treatment. A baby plant forms at a stem node. It should be left on the stem until proper roots have formed, however long this takes (up to 10 months). Then the stem should be cut above and below the keiki, leaving a little stem above, and the keiki can be potted. A special preparation is available that induces a plant to produce keikis.

Its almost year-round growth makes *Phalaenopsis* an ideal candidate for Seramis or

Paphiopedilum lawrenceanum *comes originally from northern Borneo, where it grows on the ground in forest shade. This plant should never be allowed to become dry.*

hydroculture. The plant forms so-called terminal buds. If the flowers aren't pollinated – which is usually the case indoors – then one, two or three new flowers form at the tip of each flower stem after the first flowering has finished. But if you prune the spray back to the third or fourth node, the plant will develop a new spray of flowers, which will grow for about three months and then start flowering again. This means you shouldn't remove the whole stem until it has become dry and yellow.

## *Paphiopedilum* Slipper orchids

This genus contains about 70 species from both colder and warmer parts of Asia. Slipper orchids are popular not only because they flower for so long but because they are easy to look after. At one time they were much better known than the moth orchid. Slipper orchids became houseplants before the advent of central heating, when it was impossible to keep a room warm enough for a *Phalaenopsis*.

- *P. insigne* is a typical slipper orchid, growing in sunny positions on limestone cliffs at altitudes of around 2,000 m (6,500 ft) in Nepal. It does well in a cold but frost-free

*One of the so-called large-flowered* Paphiopedilum *hybrids that were once very popular for cut flowers. Glorious specimens like this one can be found almost everywhere these days.*

environment. The light-green leaves are hard in texture and narrow in shape.

- *P. callosum* from Thailand and Indochina is quite different from *P. insigne*. It needs a warm, half-shaded position such as may be found in a modern living room. The leaves are broader, softer and mottled.

- *P. armeniacum*, on the other hand, is an example of the Parvisepalum group of species, which were only

*Paphiopedilum concolor grows on limestone cliffs. It ranges over a very wide area extending from Thailand across China.*

discovered in China in the late 1970s.

- Other species in this group are familiar but rarely available on the market because they are difficult to grow. They include *P. bellulatum*, *P. niveum* and *P. concolor*, all of which have more-or-less white flowers.

- The so-called primary hybrids – those created from only *Paphiopedilum* species – are different again. One example is *P.* **'Psyche'** (*P. bellulatum* × *P. niveum*). Their origins are visibly apparent, but unlike their parent plants they grow well indoors while retaining the charm of wild orchids. All *Paphiopedilum* hybrids have long-lasting flowers that usually survive for several weeks.

- Multi-flowered species, which include *P. philippinense*, *P. rothschildianum* and *P. stonei*, are normally only sold as hybrids. They produce three or more flowers on a single stem. Once you've seen them, whether the

*Paphiopedilum 'Snow Queen', like nearly all white-flowering Paphiopedilum cultivars, is the result of a cross between P. bellulatum and P. concolor. But whereas its ancestors are difficult to look after, P. 'Snow Queen' presents few problems.*

species or the hybrids, you'll want to buy them. But bear in mind that flowers use up a lot of a plant's strength, and they need to be fully grown and well fed if they are to produce flowers.

*P. philippinense*

*P. rothschildianum*

*P. stonei*

The large-flowered and multi-flowered hybrids tolerate more warmth and are therefore more suitable as houseplants.

Cultivars that were bred for cut flowers have large, mostly round flowers, but not many of them. There are a number of them on the market with open, round-shaped flowers. They are no longer any dearer than the small-flowered forms, leaving you free to choose whether you prefer size or quantity.

P. 'Pinocchio' is an example of a cultivar that produces a new flower as soon as the old flower has finished. The total flowering time may last up to six months.

**General advice**

Slipper orchids have no storage organs, but species from cooler

Paphiopedilum *'Pinocchio' is a cultivar that continually produces new flowers over a long period. It should be grown in a warm environment.*

regions need a dormant period. Most *Paphiopedilum* orchids should be kept drier in winter with more light.

- **Light:** generally less is required than for other orchids. But too little light is just as dangerous as too much, because photo-synthesis is interrupted.

- **Temperature:** these plants aren't subject to significant seasonal variation in their native habitat. However, species from cooler climes such as *P. insigne* prefer a cooler temperature at night and benefit from being kept out in the garden during the summer months. Most slipper orchids are best kept at room temperature. They don't like temperatures above 30°C (86°F) such as in a warm greenhouse or conservatory, and need to be kept shaded.

- **Substrate:** *Paphiopedilum* likes a rather finer growing medium than other orchids. Its native habitats are mostly wet throughout the year, with only a few drier months. This means it requires a damp substrate throughout the year, but it must be well drained to prevent the roots from being starved of oxygen.

Slipper orchids with simple green leaves should generally be kept cooler than those with soft, mottled leaves, the exception being the hybrids and many of the multi-flowered species.

- **Watering:** soft water is preferable. Rainwater is best, provided it isn't allowed to stand for too long, as this encourages the bacteria to multiply, leading to rotting and disease. The water should never be cold, especially in winter. Water should never be allowed to accumulate in the leaf nodes, as this also makes them rot. Very high humidity is required, particularly during the growing season, so plenty of spraying is needed.

- **Feeding:** little and often is the best regime for slipper orchids. Commercial orchid fertilisers are generally OK, although some slipper orchids such as *P. lowii* do much better with an organic fertiliser. Large plants require more feeding than those with a smaller leaf area. Plenty of new growth is required or the plant won't flower until the following season. Some forms of *Paphiopedilum* need a six-monthly dose of chalk – about a teaspoonful (5 ml) of chalk per 10-cm pot. The chalk is washed into the substrate by the water and is gradually absorbed.

- **Repotting:** this should be done every other year – or preferably every year. *Paphiopedilum* prefers a smaller pot. Slipper orchids should only be divided if they fall apart naturally, because they won't tolerate any tearing or damage to the roots. No plant tissue should ever be needlessly damaged, as rot can so easily set in. Any accidental damage should be treated with charcoal powder. Large plants produce proportionally more flowers, so it's best not to divide the plant if at all possible.

- **Pests and diseases:** all slipper orchids are vulnerable to red spider mite, which is often discovered too late, especially on mottled leaves, so continual checking is essential. Other pests are rare, though bacterial and fungal infections are quite common; plenty of fresh air is

the best way to prevent these. Some species need extra chalk; information on this is available from more specialist books.

## Cattleya

This genus includes species characterised by particularly large and beautiful flowers, often of the typical *Cattleya* shade – a kind of lilac-pink or magenta.

About 35 species are known. Most are epiphytic, though a few are lithophytic, i.e. they grow on rocks.

Cattleya aclandiae *comes from Brazil. Although found in most books on orchids, it is rarely found in collections. This probably has something to do with the climate of its homeland, which is hot and relatively dry.*

× Laeliocattleya *'Irene Finney' was created in 1964 by a Mr Hausermann in the United States. It is popularly used for cut flowers.*

*Cattleya* species also have large, swollen pseudobulbs ranging in size from 15 cm (6 in) in the case of *C. luteola* to 80 cm (32 in) in *C. guttata*. Each pseudobulb is protected by a straw-like sheath around the base, and is crowned by one or two firm, leathery, almost succulent leaves. All species grow sympodially, which means that all new shoots develop from the pseudobulbs.

- Among the most typical species is the autumn-flowering *C. labiata*, with its large, more-or-less lilac-pink flowers measuring 18 cm (7 in) across. There are five flowers on each flower stem, and the lip of the flower is mainly yellow with purple veins. Similar species to this include

*C. mossiae* (spring-flower-ing), *C. maxima* (autumn), *C. trianaei* (winter) and *C. percivaliana* (autumn). These are the most important species in cultivation.

- Among the smaller-flowered species are *C. bowringiana* and *C. skinneri*, which nonetheless have flowers measuring 7 cm (3 in) across. Both are easy to look after and produce a glorious pro-fusion of flowers, with up to 30 blooms on a single spray.

- Other smaller-flowered species such as *C. aclandiae* have flowers with a diameter of 8 cm (3 in). The latter species, in contrast to *C. bowringiana*, produces yellowish-green flowers with reddish-brown speckles.

  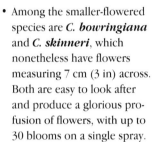

*Cattleya* is closely related to other genera such as *Laelia*, *Sophronitis*, *Brassavola* and *Epidendrum*, and it has been crossed with these to produce a vast number of hybrids (see page 82). They boast longer-lasting flowers of differing

Cattleya bowringiana *from Guatemala flowers frequently and profusely. This species was named after the English gardening enthusiast J. C. Bowring.*

shades, greater tolerance of temperature changes, and improved growth characteris-tics. Thus we not only have the typical lilac-pink flowers, but also red, yellow, green and multi-coloured blooms.

The downside of *Cattleya* species is that the flowers don't last very long, whereas most modern cultivars will flower for several weeks.

### General advice

With most varieties the dormant period is as important to observe as the light conditions, which should be bright or even sunny after a period of adjust-ment. Some of the intergeneric hybrids need warmth through-

Every new *Cattleya* should be checked carefully for mealy bugs. The sheath around the pseudo-bulb is much loved by mealy bugs and scale insects, and should be examined with extra care. You can remove the sheath very carefully and deal with the bugs by painting the area with an oil-based preparation such as Eradicoat.

out the year, during which they flower several times.

- **Light:** full morning sun if possible, not providing shade (if necessary) until noon. The attractive dark-green leaves will turn a gentle shade of red in the sunlight, and full flowering potential will be

Cattleya *has been crossed with other genera to create hybrids with flowers of all shapes, sizes and colours. The miniature varieties are of particular interest.*

*The Cattleya flower bud develops for several months inside a sheath, where it sometimes becomes trapped. If the humidity is low, the outer sheath dries out too quickly and stifles the bud. But there is a way of preventing this: when the bud becomes clearly visible (left), open the sheath carefully and the flower will carry on developing undisturbed (right).*

bowls make good containers. *Cattleya* is modest in its requirements, so grows very well on a mount.

- **Pests and diseases:** watch out for slugs on varieties with large, soft flowers. The buds sometimes produce a sticky, sugary solution just before opening. This is to attract ants, which protect the buds from other insects in the wild. However, ants should be avoided as they tend to bring other pests with them.

### Cymbidium

The name of this genus means 'boat-like' in Greek, referring to the fact that these orchids have a boat-shaped lip. Most of them are epiphytic, while a few are terrestrial. Their profusion of large, long-lasting flowers has made them the largest group of orchids to be cultivated for cut flowers.

They are also available at reasonable prices as pot plants, which are readily purchased. However, their large size means they are not best suited to pots. Most of these 'pot plants' are in fact varieties that have gone out of fashion and that are therefore no longer sought after for cut flowers. Plants used for cut

achieved. Light-green leaves are a sign of inadequate light. Growing outdoors is recommended in the summer.

- **Temperature:** depending on their country of origin, most species and hybrids grow in temperate regions, with a minimum of 12°C (54°F) during the dormant period.
- **Substrate:** firmly structured.

If the dormant period isn't observed, *Cattleya* simply carries on producing more pseudobulbs. These become continually smaller, fail to ripen and flowering ceases. The plant eventually wears itself out completely.

- **Watering:** *Cattleya* should be kept dry rather than moist, and requires more nutrients than other orchids. Don't water until the substrate has dried out.
- **Repotting:** don't repot until the pot becomes overcrowded – about once every three years. Before repotting, wait until new roots become visible. To avoid damaging the roots, plunge the pot into lukewarm water about 10 minutes beforehand. The roots will then be more supple and will slide out of the pot more easily. When dividing a plant, leave at least four pseudobulbs on each plant. All dead roots should be removed completely. Wooden baskets and shallow

flowers are planted out or cultivated in massive containers, and afterwards divided and sold as 'small' pot plants. The strength of the flowers comes from the strong annual growth of the plant, and the proportions work well. Thus *Cymbidium* hybrids make good candidates for larger pots.

**A word of advice**

With late-flowering hybrids the first flowering (on purchase) is usually the last, which is a

*Miniature* Cymbidium *hybrids produce lots of flowers and are more tolerant of warmth, so they make good house-plants. Larger specimens flower more profusely, so it's best not to divide them.*

shame, because most *Cymbidium* varieties will flower again provided they are looked after properly. So it's a good idea to buy one of the early-flowering varieties, i.e. those that in this country flower up to Christmas. The growth leading to flowering occurs in the late summer, when the plants will grow very well in the open air.

Never buy plants with too many unopened buds, as they will survive the upheaval better with at least a third of the buds in flower. When you get them home, put them in the brightest place you can and don't move them again during flowering.

If you're looking for a smaller plant, take care with the so-called **miniature *Cymbidium* hybrids**, because 'miniature' may just as easily refer to the small size of the flowers on an otherwise large plant as to the actual growth habit of the plant.

Of the 50 or so wild species, the following are the ancestors of the large-flowered varieties:

• *C. giganteum* produces yellowish-green flowers with red stripes, and grows in the western Himalayas at altitudes of around 1,800 m (6,000 ft).

*This* Cymbidium lowianum *hybrid with its large, elegant, long-lasting blooms makes an ideal candidate for a cool conservatory.*

• *C. lowianum* is very similar, as is *C. tracyanum* from Myanmar (Burma). The latter has beautifully scented flowers, though unfortunately they don't last very long.

There are some *Cymbidium* hybrids that don't grow very large and that prefer a warmer environment, making them better suited as houseplants. Their main parent species is *C. floribundum* (syn. *C. pumilum*). They develop large, overhanging (or sometimes upright) sprays of small flowers. They come in many different colours and look especially attractive in bowls.

**General advice**

The native habitats of *Cymbidium* species provide some clues

Cymbidium *'Vanguard' is a typical cut-flower variety. It must grow big in order to flower effectively, but large plants occupy a lot of space.*

as to how these orchids should be looked after.

- **Temperature:** most *Cymbidium* hybrids prefer cooler temperatures, so are not the best houseplants. They need warm days and cold nights in order to flower. All *Cymbidium* plants should preferably be kept out of doors in the summer, and in the case of early-flowering varieties this helps to promote flowering.

- **Light:** in the summer, place the plants in the shade of trees where they receive plenty of morning sun. They make ideal plants for a cool conservatory, flowering in the autumn, winter and spring while *Citrus*, *Clivia* and *Bougainvillea* are resting.

- **Substrate:** the miniatures like a finer growing medium than the large-flowered varieties. All *Cymbidium* plants

need plenty of fertiliser during the growth season, and should never be allowed to dry out. The dormant period is short, with only a slight drop in temperature, and some miniatures will carry on flowering without interruption. Don't move the plant while it's still in bud – wait until it has begun flowering.

- **Watering:** this is needed throughout the year, though plants can be left unwatered for just a few weeks in winter. One important exception is after repotting, when for two weeks they should be sprayed instead of being watered.

- **Feeding:** add fertiliser every third time you water.

- **Repotting:** as the plants grow almost all year round, they should be repotted when flowering is over and divided if necessary, though undivided plants will produce a better display of flowers.

- **Pests and diseases:** pay particular attention to snails while these plants are in the garden. *Cymbidium* is also a frequent martyr to red spider mite and scale insects, but biological controls will be very effective either indoors or in a conservatory.

### *Odontoglossum*

The name comes from the Greek and means 'tooth tongue', which is a reference to the tooth-like features on the lip. There are generally thought to be about 100 species of *Odontoglossum*, although the genus is continually being reclassified. Many species have, for example, been consigned to the related genus *Oncidium* (see page 74). This lack of clarity points to a genus that can be easily crossed with other genera.

- The first species to flower in Europe (in 1836) was **O. bictoniense**, now known as

Lemboglossum bictoniense *is often sold under its old name* Odontoglossum bictoniense. *It makes an excellent houseplant.*

*Lemboglossum bictoniense*, which grows at altitudes of between 1,500 and 3,000 m (5,000–10,000 ft) in the mountain rainforests of Mexico, Guatemala and El Salvador. The flower stems may grow up to 1 m (40 in) in height. The individual flowers measure some 4 cm (1.5 in) across, and vary in colour between pink and magenta, with a lighter-coloured lip.

- The most important species is *O. crispum*. No other orchid has had so much money spent on it, or has been the subject of more collecting expeditions – or more legends. Britain was for many years the land of the *Odontoglossum*. This orchid's attractive, gently overhanging sprays grow up to 60 cm (24 in) long. Each is made up of 30 or more flowers up to 7 cm (3 in) across. They are white with faint traces of pink or yellow, and dark spots or speckles. Lots of different names have been given to the many naturally occurring varieties, with their different colours and shapes.

- Many well-known members of the genus, including *O. grande*, *O. insleayi* and *O. williamsianum*, have been reassigned to the genus *Rossioglossum*, though they are often better known under their old name. Perhaps the most important of these species is the **clown orchid** (*R. grande* syn. *O. grande*). The individual flowers are up to 10 cm (4 in) across, and are mainly yellow with rows of reddish-brown spots and a 'clown' pattern on the lip (see page 20). This was one of the first orchids to become popular as a houseplant.

- Yet another genus that has been carved out of *Odontoglossum* is *Lemboglossum*. *L. cervantesii* and *L. rossii*, which both come from Mexico, are both still commonly called by their old name in the literature.

### General advice

- **Temperature:** *Odontoglossum* should not be kept too warm. All the well-known species thrive in cool temper-

*Lemboglossum bictoniense* (syn. *Odontoglossum bictoniense*) flowers long and faithfully. It is also easy to look after, making it the ideal orchid for a beginner.

atures, although intergeneric hybrids (e.g. × *Odontioda*) prefer a more temperate situation. *Odontoglossum* also does well in the garden during the summer. Always observe the dormant period, when shade is essential.

- **Watering:** spray frequently to ensure plenty of humidity.

- **Repotting:** if necessary, repot early in the year, well before the new shoots begin, because the new roots start to form about four weeks before the shoots.

*Odontoglossum crispum is probably the most famous orchid of legend.*

Lemboglossum rossii – *better known as* Odontoglossum rossii – *came originally from Mexico. A true miniature orchid, it is not easy to look after and is sensitive to waterlogging.*

*× Odontonia 'Fiona Isler' is strikingly similar to Lemboglossum bictoniense except that it has more vigorous sprays of bigger flowers.*

- **Pests and diseases:** red spider mite are as much of a problem as with other orchids, and are often spotted too late. As soon as you notice the slightest sign of infestation, apply biological controls immediately (see page 42). Herbal brews (see page 45) may help ward off fungal disease.

*Odontoglossum* has been crossed with other genera with the aim of producing a larger range of even more beautiful orchids. The most successful crossings were with *Cochlioda*, which contains only five species, the most important one for hybrids being *C. noezliana*. The new genus that resulted was called × *Odontioda* (see page 84).

### Oncidium

*Oncidium* is closely related to *Odontoglossum*. It is an extensive genus, with more than 500 species, most of which are epiphytes from Central and South America. Some live in warm, humid regions, while others live close to permanent snow.

There are both large and small species, both with and without pseudobulbs. The flowers are equally varied, though they mostly form large sprays, sometimes with hundreds of individual flowers. The commonest colour is yellow, with brown or greenish speckles or stripes. The flower sprays often look like swarms of insects, and this alone causes male insects to brush against the flowers and pollinate them in the process.

- The **butterfly orchid (O. papilio)** and the closely related **O. kramerianum** both have flowers that look like butterflies (the Americans call the whole genus butterfly orchids). The flowers seem to float in the air with their long 'antennae', seemingly independent of the plants. New flowers are continually forming at the tip of each spray. Both species come from the lower slopes of their native

*The flowers of the butterfly orchid (Oncidium papilio) are what gave the orchid its name.*

mountain forests, and should be kept correspondingly warm.

- **O. concolor** from Brazil has only small flowers measuring some 3 cm (1 in) across, but makes up for this with large sprays, often with 30 flowers apiece. This species should not be kept too moist and will tolerate dry air.

- **O. altissimum** from the West Indies is a very much bigger plant, with pseudobulbs and leaves that together measure

up to 40 cm (16 in). The flower stems may be up to 3 m (10 ft) long, and form branching sprays covered with small yellow flowers. This irrepressible plant will flower at both higher and lower temperatures.

- **O. leucochilum**, which grows in both dry and wet forests in Mexico, Honduras and Guatemala, is a species that flowers better if the stems are pruned. The flowers are not yellow, but whitish-green with red-brown speckles and a white lip. This plant does well in any room, and doesn't need much light. The flowers will last for several weeks.

- **O. ornithorhynchum** is also worth mentioning. Its profuse sprays of small flowers give off a strong scent. The flower stems are gently overhanging, and each flower is lilac-pink with yellow callus formations on the lip. Originating in Mexico and Guatemala, this species doesn't require much warmth but is very adaptable except

*Oncidium ornithorhynchum produces hosts of small, beautifully designed flowers and is noted for its strong scent.*

during the dormant phase, when it must be kept cool and dry.

- **O. tigrinum** is from Mexico. The flowers are striped yellow and brown like a tiger – hence the specific name. They measure 6 cm (2.5 in) across and are carried on branching sprays that grow up to 1 m (40 in) long. Some varieties have different yellow-and-brown patterns,

*Oncidium papilio* (butterfly orchid) and *O. kramerianum* are not easy plants to look after, and require a warm rather than a temperate environment. A hybrid of the two species, *O.* Kalihii, is easier to cultivate and is therefore sold more often.

and new cultivars have been developed from them. This particular species has been crossed with *Odontoglossum* species, the resulting genus being × *Odontocidium* (see page 84).

**General advice**

- **Light:** most *Oncidium* species don't need any more

If an *Oncidium* spray grows too long indoors, it can be pruned to any length you like. About five to seven weeks later the spray will form branches from that point and develop new flowers. Always assume that the plant will continue flowering provided the sprays don't become dry.

light than *Phalaenopsis*, the only exception being those with thick succulent leaves, which need even more light than *Cattleya*. Hybrids with *Miltonia* (× *Miltonidium*) have lighter-coloured leaves and require less light.

- **Substrate:** most *Oncidium* species have fine roots, and require a firmly structured but fine growing medium. They react badly to water-logging. *Oncidium* species from mountain regions need some extra chalk in the substrate, which should be allowed to dry out properly before it is watered.

- **Watering:** avoid waterlogging at all costs. The use of herbal brews (see page 45) can stop the roots from rotting.

- **Feeding:** most *Oncidium* species should have the same feeding regime as other orchids. However, species with lighter-coloured leaves require fewer nutrients.

- **Repotting:** repot immediately when growth begins, as the roots react badly to being disturbed. When dividing, don't go for plants that are too small.

- **Pests:** watch out for red spider mite and scale insects.

## Miltoniopsis/Miltonia
**Pansy orchids**

Pansy orchids were originally all called *Miltonia*, but subsequent studies led to these plants being split into two distinct genera: *Miltonia* is now restricted to Brazilian species, which have distinct characteristics, and the rest are *Miltoniopsis*. However, you may still find both kinds referred to as *Miltonia*.

The vigorous houseplants that we nowadays think of as typical *Miltonia* are in fact a modern creation – the result of crossing fast-growing Brazilian species with more delicate species from the cloud-forest regions.

Modern pansy orchids are characterised by clear, strong flower colours. Yellow, pink and white-flowered varieties make particularly effective house-plants. The often interesting lip formation on a *Miltonia* flower is also known as the 'mask'.

Perhaps the most famous hybrid group is ***Miltonia* Celle**, which was created in Germany. It includes such well-known cultivars as *M.* Celle 'Wasserfall', *M.* Celle 'Feuerwerk', *M.* Celle 'Hamburg', *M.* Celle 'Hannover' and *M.* Celle 'Baden Baden' – the ancestors of varieties to be found all over the world.

*Miltonia* Celle *is the best-known group of pansy orchid hybrids, developed in Germany in 1958.*

### General advice

The pansy orchids that are sold as houseplants are generally unproblematic. They are tolerant of warmth, and the flowers are extremely long-lasting. The plant is simple to cultivate, because it grows practically all year round and hardly requires a dormant period.

*Miltonia* flowers survive for a long time, but their size and the intensity of their colours depends on how much light they receive, so that winter blooms are inevitably less impressive. If well cared for, a pansy orchid will produce a new flower every eight months.

When a flower has finished, cut the stem off cleanly, taking care not to pull or tear it. As long as the stem is green, it stays firmly attached to the pseudobulb.

- **Light:** pansy orchids react badly to too much light. The light-green leaves take on a reddish tinge that varies depending on the cultivar, and that can eventually lead to irreparable burns.

- **Watering:** the thin roots are sensitive to too much or too little moisture, and much prefer an even supply. If the plant gets too wet or too dry, growth is temporarily halted. Continual stopping and starting leads to concertina-like growth in the leaves (see page 39). If the problem occurs with a soft new shoot, then the whole shoot may even die.

- **Feeding:** pansy orchids should be fed the normal amount for orchids in general. Fast growth and vigorous flowers use up plenty of nutrients. However, you need to prevent the fertiliser solution from coming into direct contact with the roots, because they are sensitive to salts, including those in the fertiliser.

- **Pests and diseases:** rotting can be caused by overwatering and affects the soft leaves in particular. Scale insects often nest between the pseudobulbs and in the base of the pseudobulbs. As pansy orchids don't like oil-based products such as Eradicoat, it's best to use soap or biological controls. The same applies to red spider mite,

*Miltonia spectabilis* var. moreliana *from Brazil is the ideal orchid for beginners, being extremely tolerant of faulty treatment or inappropriate temperatures.*

Laelia harpophylla *comes from Brazil. The intense flower colour is found in many yellow hybrids where the species has been crossed with* Cattleya.

Experience suggests that many *Laelia* species suffer from a shortage of trace elements, which leads to unsatisfactory development in the plant. This problem can be avoided by adding loam to the substrate. Its nutrients will only be absorbed gradually, so if you need a more immediate solution, use a specific fertiliser that contains trace elements. Such feeds are available in liquid or powder form.

which attacks the soft leaves; this can be dealt with, either indoors or in a greenhouse, by means of predatory mites.

## Laelia

*Laelia* species are found in a broad range extending southwards from Mexico to Peru and Brazil. Their requirements vary according to the region they come from. About 60 species are known, of which many are epiphytic, some terrestrial and

some lithophytic. Lithophytes are much the same as epiphytes except that they live on rock or scree instead of tree branches. Such a situation is difficult to imitate in cultivation. Rock stores plenty of heat but very little moisture. It also provides extra minerals, which means that lithophytic plants in cultivation can often suffer from a shortage of trace elements. The problem can be rectified with a fertiliser that contains extra trace elements.

- *L. milleri* is a lithophytic orchid from Brazil. It's a very robust plant, with small orange-red flowers measuring 5 cm (2 in) across.

- *L. liliputiana* also comes originally from Brazil. It is much smaller, with pseudo-bulbs only 1 cm (0.4 in) tall and leaves only 2 cm (0.8 in) long. But the flowers measure 3 cm (1 in) across.

- *L. purpurata* is a real beauty that has become the national flower of Brazil. The flowers, which measure 15 cm (5 in) across, are white to light pink in colour, while the lip is deep purple at the base with purple veins running towards the tip. Each flower spray may contain up to six blooms. This species comes in many different varieties with, for example, white flowers with orange lips, or pink flowers with red lips. Many orchid collections in Brazil are devoted to *L. purpurata* alone, and there are annual exhibitions with awards.

- *L. pumila*, again from Brazil, is a dwarf species. Although it grows to only 15 cm (6 in), its flowers measure 11 cm (4 in) across (they are magenta with a purple groove in the lip). Truly a giant among dwarfs!

- Two more Brazilian species are worth noting: *L. cinnabarina* and *L. harpophylla*. Both grow in more temperate conditions and flower in winter. Their descendants are characterised by clear colours and long-lasting flowers.

- The three species *L. anceps*, *L. autumnalis* and *L. gouldiana* all come from Mexico. Their elegant flowers are borne on long stems, and are pinkish lilac with a darker lip. They shouldn't be kept too warm, although *L. gouldiana* will tolerate more warmth than the others.

- *L. autumnalis* is known in Mexico as the *flor de todos los Santos* or 'All Saints' Flower' because it is used as decoration for that festival.

Because it has become very rare, attempts are being made to reintroduce cultivated plants into the wild.

The beauty and elegance of *Laelia* are also to be found among its hybrids, of which the most impressive are intergeneric crosses with *Cattleya* (see × *Laeliocattleya* on page 82).

### General advice

Treatment is similar to that for *Cattleya* (see page 69). The tall, thin pseudobulbs enable new plants to grow large indoors.

*Laelia pumila* is rather more demanding than the other species, because it always requires more humidity, whether it is grown on a mount or in a container. During the growing season it also needs plenty of water and nutrients in the substrate. Strict observation of the dormant period is essential, though the same is true of many *Laelia* species.

One exceptional species is *L. purpurata*, which likes extreme conditions. It thrives on plenty of light, high daytime temperatures and low night temperatures, and needs to be kept very humid while growing but extremely dry while dormant.

## Hybrids – orchids of mixed parentage

Of all the orchids that are available on the market as pot plants or houseplants, the overwhelming proportion are hybrids, and most of these hybrids are intergeneric, having been derived from more than one naturally occurring genus.

Unfortunately, many flower shops and garden centres tend to provide wrong or incomplete names. And if a plant name is given wrongly, then it becomes difficult to work out the correct treatment, or to find out more useful information about a particular plant.

Admittedly, if your plant is a moth orchid (*Phalaenopsis*), you don't need to know its exact origins in order to work out the correct treatment. But it's a rather different case with a slipper orchid, for example, where you haven't been given the botanical name.

Even more confusing are those brightly coloured specimens with white, yellow or red

*x Odontocidium 'Hansueli Isler' – a successful hybrid from Switzerland – is easy to look after, with long-lasting flowers, but you do need to watch out for red spider mite.*

flowers and a catch-all name such as 'Cambria'.

In fact there are very few genuine Cambria varieties available, of which the commonest is × *Vuylstekeara* Cambria 'Plush' FCC/RHS (see page 58) – an especially prestigious form of the original 1931 cultivar that has survived in small numbers through the division of just a few plants. Thanks to the advent of meristem reproduction (tissue culture), this once rare variety has now become widely available, while mutations have provided yet other forms of Cambria. However, many orchids that are sold as 'Cambria' have totally different forebears, while some even belong to totally different genera.

As you start to become familiar with orchids, you will quickly discover that there are vast numbers of different orchids available that require very little effort to look after provided they are kept at the right temperature. Moreover, the great majority of these will be intergeneric hybrids, where the combination of the very different characteristics of the parent species has created plants that are particularly tolerant and adaptable.

## The most important hybrids

Most orchids on the market are cultivated forms, the majority of which are hybrids. The choice varies greatly from one garden centre to another, so if you want a specific cultivar, you are better advised to contact a specialist supplier (some suppliers provide a delivery service).

You should be able to find the orchids listed below in flower shops, garden centres or orchid nurseries, though not all may be available at any particular time, and you may find that varieties are not always identified unless you use an orchid nursery. Some of those listed below may only be available at orchid nurseries.

### *Ascocentrum* and × *Ascocenda*

× *Ascocenda* is a hybrid of *Ascocentrum* × *Vanda*. The best-known variety is × *Ascocenda* 'Meda Arnold', which has flowers ranging from violet to red. Red forms originate mainly from purely *Ascocentrum* species. Many of the specimens on sale arrive in wooden baskets from the Far East. As they only grow very slowly in this country, at least until the first flowering, most are actually grown in the Far East. Fresh imports have no substrate apart from a little coir in the basket, so the roots are simply growing in the open air.

### Treatment

These orchids need lots of humidity in order to grow properly as houseplants. Daily spraying is essential – several times a day in the summer. Spraying enables both the leaves and the roots to absorb nutrients. Transplanting is only necessary if the wooden basket disintegrates.

*Ascocentrum ampullaceum grows to just 30 cm (12 in) tall with flowers that grow straight from the leaf stem. This species comes mainly from Thailand. It needs plenty of warmth and light, and must never be allowed to become dry.*

*× Sophrolaeliocattleya 'Dark Waters' is a long name for a relatively small plant. This hybrid was first created in 1962, and is still occasionally on sale.*

## Brassia and its hybrids

Apart from the occasional instance of × *Miltassia* (*Miltonia × Brassia*), the commonest hybrid available is *Brassia* 'Rex', which is descended from *B. verrucosa*, a species with large, spidery flowers.

Large-flowered hybrids are in general less long-flowering than small-flowered ones. You should always bear this in mind when buying orchids.

## Treatment

These vigorous plants will only flower if they are allowed to rest for long enough. They also need plenty of feeding.

## Cattleya and its hybrids

Plants that are sold as *Cattleya* are pure *Cattleya* hybrids. Their main flower colour is lilac, or occasionally white.

Crosses with *Brassavola* are known as × *Brassocattleya*. They are not very common these days, but a few old varieties are available. Their intoxicatingly sweet scent is particularly striking. The flowers are large and white with a fringed lip, but don't last very long. This plant needs a lot of light.

× *Laeliocattleya* needs similar treatment to *Cattleya*; miniature forms need more light.

× *Brassolaeliocattleya* hybrids are little different from ordinary *Cattleya*, and require similar care.

× *Sophrocattleya* is a hybrid of *Sophronitis × Cattleya*. The small, deep-red flowers of *Sophronitis* lend their colour to × *Sophrocattleya*, but most hybrids are smaller in habit. Small-flowered varieties tolerate

lower temperatures. They grow continuously and require only a short rest period.

× *Sophrolaeliocattleya* involves yet another parent genus – *Laelia* – but should be treated similarly to *Cattleya*. Like × *Sophrocattleya*, it includes many small, vigorous, long-lasting plants.

× *Potinara* has as many as four parent genera – *Brassavola × Cattleya × Laelia × Sophronitis* – but requires the same treatment as *Cattleya*.

## Cymbidium hybrids

*Cymbidium* hybrids all derive from species within the same genus. Genuine miniatures from Australia are now becoming available as pot plants, though they can also be grown in window troughs.

## Dendrobium hybrids

There is an important distinction between *D. nobile* hybrids and *D. phalaenopsis* hybrids.

### D. nobile hybrids

The parent species, *D. nobile*, ranges across southern Asia

Dendrobium nobile *hybrids have become much better known in recent years, thanks mainly to the efforts of Japanese growers.*

from India to China via Laos and Vietnam.

**Treatment**

During the dormant period, *D. nobile* hybrids lose their foliage from the previous year's growth. They make good houseplants as they are generally undemanding with regard to temperature. However, they need to be kept cooler during the dormant period.

The new flowers will not appear until the leaves have dropped. The flowers vary in colour from white to lilac, with yellow and red too, and the lip is usually of a contrasting colour.

### D. phalaenopsis hybrids

The specific name points to the fact that the flowers are similar to those of the moth orchid. The parent species is found in Queensland, Australia, and on the islands of New Guinea, Moluccas and Timor.

The pseudobulbs may grow as long as 60 cm (24 in) and the flowers grow on 50-cm (20-in) long stems. They are usually purple, although some are pink. They are perhaps most familiar as cut flowers imported daily from Singapore and Bangkok. The cut flowers will last several weeks, although the plants themselves will last very much longer. Pot plants have been produced from hybrids with smaller species.

**Treatment**

*D. phalaenopsis* hybrids generally pose no problems as houseplants, though they need to be kept drier during the dormant season. As with moth orchids (see page 64), the buds may sometimes be affected by shortage of light, turning yellow and eventually dropping off. There is no real solution to this problem because artificial light doesn't help. It's best to try again in the next growing season, as plants that fail to flower tend to flower more vigorously next time round.

### × Doritaenopsis

× *Doritaenopsis* hybrids, from *Phalaenopsis* × *Doritis*, are little different from *Phalaenopsis* in terms of care, except that the leaves, being leathery, will tolerate more light and dryness. These hybrids may flower for even longer than *Phalaenopsis*, although they don't flower a second time in the season.

### × Miltonidium

× *Miltonidium* hybrids (*Miltonia* × *Oncidium*) are just some of the many *Miltonia* hybrids

Dendrobium phalaenopsis *is similar to the moth orchid in that it reacts badly to being moved after purchase. In order to avoid this, it's best to buy plants that are almost completely in flower.*

that are being developed in the USA, and that promise to improve on older varieties. However, they are very expensive as they grow very slowly. The flowering period lasts for several weeks.

### × *Odontioda*

× *Odontioda*, a hybrid from *Odontoglossum × Cochlioda*,

× Odontocidium *'Susan Kaufman' produces a mass of flowers that amply compensates for their small size. This variety is easy to grow but should not be kept too moist.*

has already been mentioned (see page 74) and is generally only available from orchid specialists. Its flowers are particularly interesting and attractive, being round or star-shaped, with colours ranging from white to pink, lilac, red and yellow, and often with purple spots or stripes. It needs to be grown in cool, humid conditions.

### Other hybrids from the *Oncidium* group

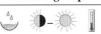

- × *Vuylstekeara* is the best-known hybrid genus in the *Oncidium* group. It arose from the three genera *Cochlioda*, *Miltonia/Miltoniopsis* and *Odontoglossum* (see also page 58). Originally developed to bring colour into *Odontoglossum crispum* hybrids, it turned out to have better growing characteristics too. You shouldn't keep it too warm, and you should beware of red spider mite if the humidity is reduced. Hang it in the garden during the summer, and transplant every other year.

- × *Odontocidium* (*Odontoglossum × Oncidium*) grows

× Odontonia *'Susan Bogdanow' demonstrates that not everything that looks like a* Miltonia *is a* Miltonia. *Despite its complex name, it is not difficult to look after.*

very easily. Varieties such as 'Wintergold' and 'Juno' show a visible resemblance to *Oncidium*, having small, mainly yellow flowers with brown stripes. The large-flowered cultivars are more like their *Odontoglossum* ancestors, and need a cooler environment.

- × *Odontonia* is the result of *Odontoglossum × Miltonia*. The best-known example is × *Odontonia* Boussole 'Blanche', which has white flowers with bright-red spots. × *Odontonia* hybrids require much the same treatment as × *Vuylstekeara* (see above). They can grow quite fast, producing a new flower every eight months.

- **× Wilsonara** unites three genera: *Oncidium* × *Odontoglossum* × *Cochlioda*. The flowers are like those of × *Odontioda* but it grows more vigorously. Most varieties have yellow or yellow-brown flowers. *Oncidium tigrinum* is an important parent species. The cultivar × *Wilsonara* 'Tiger Brew' is readily available.

- **× Burrageara** is the result when a fourth genus – *Miltonia* – is crossed with those of × *Wilsonara*. The flowers are again similar to those of × *Vuylstekeara*. Red and orange-yellow varieties are generally available for purchase. They flower readily and are easy to look after indoors.

## A summary of the hybrids from the *Oncidium* group

The table opposite includes all the hybrid genera that you are likely to find in garden centres or orchid nurseries, together with the parent genera. The international abbreviations are given in brackets.

| Summary of the hybrids from the *Oncidium* group | |
|---|---|
| × *Bakerara* (*Bak.*) | *Brassia* (*Brs.*) × *Miltonia* (*Milt.*) × *Odontoglossum* (*Odm*) × *Oncidium* (*Onc.*) |
| × *Baldwinara* (*Bdwna*) | *Aspasia* (*Asp.*) × *Cochlioda* (*Cda*) × *Odontoglossum* (*Odm*) × *Oncidium* (*Onc.*) |
| × *Beallara* (*Bllra*) | *Brassia* (*Brs.*) × *Cochlioda* (*Cda*) × *Miltonia* (*Milt.*) × *Odontoglossum* (*Odm*) |
| × *Biltonara* (*Bilt.*) | *Ada* (*Ada*) × *Cochlioda* (*Cda*) × *Miltonia* (*Milt.*) × *Odontoglossum* (*Odm.*) |
| × *Brassidium* (*Brsdm*) | *Brassia* (*Brs.*) × *Oncidium* (*Onc.*) |
| × *Brassioda* (*Broda*) | *Brassia* (*Brs.*) × *Cochlioda* (*Cda*) |
| × *Burrageara* (*Burr.*) | *Cochlioda* (*Cda*) × *Miltonia* (*Milt.*) × *Odontoglossum* (*Odm*) × *Oncidium* (*Onc.*) |
| × *Colmanara* (*Colm.*) | *Miltonia* (*Milt.*) × *Odontoglossum* (*Odm*) × *Oncidium* (*Onc.*) |
| × *Duggerara* (*Dugg.*) | *Ada* (*Ada*) × *Brassia* (*Brs.*) × *Miltonia* (*Milt.*) |
| × *Maclellanara* (*Mclna*) | *Brassia* (*Brs.*) × *Odontoglossum* (*Odm*) × *Oncidium* (*Onc.*) |
| × *Miltadium* (*Mtadm*) | *Ada* (*Ada*) × *Miltonia* (*Milt.*) × *Oncidium* (*Onc.*) |
| × *Miltassia* (*Mtssa*) | *Brassia* (*Brs.*) × *Miltonia* (*Milt.*) |
| × *Miltonidium* (*Mtdm*) | *Miltonia* (*Milt.*) × *Oncidium* (*Onc.*) |
| × *Miltonioda* (*Mtda*) | *Cochlioda* (*Cda*) × *Miltonia* (*Milt.*) |
| × *Odontioda* (*Oda*) | *Cochlioda* (*Cda*) × *Odontoglossum* (*Odm*) |
| × *Odontobrassia* (*Odbrs.*) | *Brassia* (*Brs.*) × *Odontoglossum* (*Odm*) |
| × *Odontocidium* (*Odcdm*) | *Odontoglossum* (*Odm*) × *Oncidium* (*Onc.*) |
| × *Odontonia* (*Odtna*) | *Miltonia* (*Milt.*) × *Odontoglossum* (*Odm*) |
| × *Odontorettia* (*Odrta*) | *Comparettia* (*Comp.*) × *Odontoglossum* (*Odm*) |
| × *Vuylstekeara* (*Vuyl.*) | *Cochlioda* (*Cda*) × *Miltonia* (*Milt.*) × *Odontoglossum* (*Odm*) |
| × *Warneara* (*Wnra*) | *Comparettia* (*Comp.*) × *Oncidium* (*Onc.*) × *Rodriguezia* (*Rdza*) |
| × *Wilsonara* (*Wils.*) | *Cochlioda* (*Cda*) × *Odontoglossum* (*Odm*) × *Oncidium* (*Onc.*) |

# Species orchids

The following selection of species plants may be available from outlets in the UK, though you are more likely to find them at specialist orchid nurseries. All of them have been bred from cultivated stock or reproduced by division.

### *Aërides odorata*

**Origins:** Tropical Asia
**Treatment:** warmth and constant humidity. Prefers epiphytic cultivation. Suitable for mounting on a clay pipe.

### *Angraecum sesquipedale* Comet orchid

**Origins:** Madagascar
**Treatment:** needs plenty of fresh air, and never let it dry out. Use shallow containers. Remove side shoots.

### *Ansellia africana*

**Origins:** West Africa
**Treatment:** use shallow containers and don't transplant too often. A good tub plant for a conservatory. Place in the garden during the summer.

### *Ascocentrum miniatum*

**Origins:** Thailand, India
**Treatment:** needs plenty of light and humidity. Use a wooden basket.

### *Barkeria spectabilis*

**Origins:** Mexico, Guatemala, El Salvador
**Treatment:** choose an earthy growing medium and a shallow container. Needs good light; don't protect from the sun until the leaves are tinged with red.

### *Bifrenaria harrisoniae*

**Origins:** Brazil to Venezuela
**Treatment:** keep in the garden in the summer. Dormant period must be observed or else it won't flower.

### *Bletilla striata*

**Origins:** China, Japan
**Treatment:** described in some catalogues as a herbaceous perennial, but not properly frost-hardy in the UK. Needs a coarse, earthy substrate with extra loam. Keep dry and frost-free in the winter, preferably in a cellar, and eventually plant out in May.

### *Brassavola digbyana* (syn. *Rhyncholaelia digbyana*)

**Origins:** Honduras
**Treatment:** sunny position. Introduce gradually to the outdoors during the summer months.

### *Brassavola nodosa* Lady-of-the-night

**Origins:** Tropical America, West Indies
**Treatment:** will flower in both warm and temperate conditions. Suitable for a shaded position.

### Brassia antherotes

**Origins:** Central and eastern South America
**Treatment:** observe dormant period. Needs plenty of fertiliser. Grows vigorously.

### Brassia verrucosa

**Origins:** Central America
**Treatment:** needs plenty of light and humidity, and lots of moisture and nutrients during the growing period. Observe dormant period, but don't keep too cold.

Brassovola nodosa *is supposed to have been the first tropical orchid to come to flower in Europe. This happened in 1615.*

### Bulbophyllum medusae

**Origins:** Borneo, Malay Peninsula
**Treatment:** can be grown over the edge of a basket, using a very open substrate.

### Calanthe vestita

**Origins:** Southeast Asia
**Treatment:** plants should be grown in a nutrient-rich soil, which could even be ordinary planting compost with polystyrene chips. Repot annually when new growth begins. Water and feed regularly depending on the state of the leaves. Reduce watering when they have fully developed. Once the leaves have dropped, keep completely dry until new growth begins.

### Chysis aurea var. bractescens

**Origins:** Mexico
**Treatment:** needs plenty of light despite the light-coloured leaves. The growth season is relatively short. Plenty of water and fertiliser.

Calanthe vestita *flowers during the dormant period when all the leaves have fallen.*

### Cochleanthes discolor

**Origins:** Cuba, Honduras, Panama, Venezuela
**Treatment:** water little and often, and feed carefully. Choose a fine growing medium. Use moss for planting on a mount.

### Coelogyne cristata

**Origins:** Himalayas up to 2,000 m (6,500 ft)
**Treatment:** grow in a wooden basket. During dormant season, keep in a cool, airy position until pseudobulbs shrivel.

*The clam-shell orchid (Encyclia cochleata) produces very interesting and long-lasting flowers, and has recently become popular again as a pot plant.*

## Coelogyne massangeana

**Origins:** Assam
**Treatment:** must be grown in a wooden basket. Grows all year round, making it easy to look after. Keep moist and well fertilised, but avoid water-logging.

## Dendrobium aggregatum
### (syn. *D. lindleyi*)

**Origins:** China, India, Burma, Thailand
**Treatment:** plants do best on a mount or in a basket. Needs temperate conditions. During

the rest period, keep dry at around 8°C (46°F).

## Dendrobium chrysotoxum

**Origins:** Burma
**Treatment:** needs to be in a cooler, airier position than *D. aggregatum*, but the rest period may be observed less strictly.

## Dendrobium densiflorum
## (syn. *D. thyrsiflorum*)

**Origins:** North India, Burma
**Treatment:** needs warm, humid conditions – more temperate during the dormant period. Choose a fairly small, shallow pot.

## Dendrobium kingianum

**Origins:** Australia
**Treatment:** may be grown in all mediums and conditions – on a mount or in a pot, and warm, temperate or cold – but will only flower after a cool, dry rest period.

## Doritis pulcherrima

**Origins:** Burma, Indo-China, Sumatra
**Treatment:** this particular *Doritis* species will tolerate any well-lit position provided that it isn't kept too moist.

## Encyclia chondylobulbon

**Origins:** Mexico
**Treatment:** provide plenty of light, but keep the plant out of direct sun. This species needs to be kept dormant in the winter.

## Encyclia citrina
## (syn. *Cattleya citrina*)

**Origins:** Mexico
**Treatment:** this is rather a fussy plant that grows best on a mount in company with cactuses. It requires plenty of light, lots of water during the growing season, and strict observance of the dormant period.

### Encyclia cochleata (syn. *Epidendrum cochleatum*) Clam-shell orchid

**Origins:** Tropical America
**Treatment:** needs only a short rest period, when it should be kept dry and well lit.

### Encyclia cordigera (syn. *E. atropurpurea* syn. *Epidendrum atropurpureum*)

**Origins:** Tropical America
**Treatment:** requires strict observance of a short dormant period, during which it should be kept dry and well lit.

### Encyclia fragrans (syn. *Epidendrum fragrans*)

**Origins:** Tropical America
**Treatment:** presents no problems. Flowers well in temperate and even cooler conditions.

### Gongora galeata

**Origins:** Mexico
**Treatment:** the young shoots

are extremely vulnerable, and may easily rot or fall prey to aphids.

### Lycaste aromatica

**Origins:** Central America
**Treatment:** needs to be kept continuously moist throughout the growing season, and requires large amounts of nutrients.

### Lycaste virginalis (syn. *L. skinnerii*)

**Origins:** Central America
**Treatment:** similar requirements to those for the previous species. Because this orchid is the national flower of Guatemala, it has now become rare and is therefore protected in the wild.

### Masdevallia coccinea

**Origins:** Colombia
**Treatment:** with this particular *Masdevallia* species, the roots should be kept evenly moist but never actually wet.

*The rather small flowers of Lycaste aromatica appear just before the new shoots. Even if you fail to see them you'll be sure to notice the scent.*

### Masdevallia tovarensis

**Origins:** Venezuela
**Treatment:** similar requirements to *M. coccinea*, but generally needs to be kept warmer. The flowers bloom a second time on the previous year's growth.

### Maxillaria picta

**Origins:** Brazil
**Treatment:** a little humidity and plenty of fresh air during the rest period.

Phaius tankervilleae – *this long-forgotten species has recently made a comeback, and makes an ideal candidate for a cool conservatory.*

## Maxillaria tenuifolia

**Origins:** Central America
**Treatment:** similar requirements to those for *M. picta* (see previous page), but in general more light is required.

## Phaius tankervilliae

**Origins:** China
**Treatment:** once a popular species for cut flowers. A terrestrial plant with large, extremely interesting flowers. Similar requirements to *Cymbidium* (see page 71). Vulnerable to attack from red spider mite.

## Phragmipedium caudatum

**Origins:** Peru
**Treatment:** temperate to cool, and always humid. Grows slowly.

## Pleione formosana

**Origins:** China
**Treatment:** often misleadingly described in catalogues as a hardy herbaceous perennial, this orchid will survive cold, dry weather but not the damp cold of British winters. It can be planted out if sufficient protection is provided, but it's best to keep the pseudobulbs in the fridge over the winter and plant them out again in March. Use an earthy substrate. Thinned-out garden compost may be suitable.

## Rhynchostylis retusa

**Origins:** Tropical Asia
**Treatment:** should be grown in a basket or a bowl, using a coarse substrate.

## Sophronitis coccinea

**Origins:** Brazil
**Treatment:** an extremely adaptable plant. It's important to have an open, well-drained substrate. It likes moisture, but you should avoid waterlogging.

Spathoglottis plicata *has become a popular houseplant and is also easy to look after.*

It thrives on plenty of fresh, humid air, and should be kept in a small pot or basket. It needs plenty of light, even in winter.

## Spathoglottis plicata

**Origins:** China
**Treatment:** this orchid requires plenty of light, a fine but firmly structured substrate, and plenty of water and nutrients during the growing season. During the dormant period a temperature of 12°C (54°F) is sufficient and the plant should be given very little water.

## Stanhopea oculata

**Origins:** Central America
**Treatment:** this orchid must be grown in a basket because the flower grows downwards. From mid-May onwards, hang the basket from a tree in the garden – but don't forget to feed the plant! Don't ever let the roots dry out completely, even in winter.

## Trichopilia tortilis

**Origins:** Mexico, Guatemala, Honduras, El Salvador
**Treatment:** this species requires constant humidity and a moist substrate. It needs a minimum temperature of 15°C (59°F) during the dormant period. It works best in a basket on account of the hanging flowers.

## Vanilla planifolia
## Vanilla

**Origins:** Central America, West Indies
**Treatment:** vanilla is too big to be a pot plant, but makes an interesting plant for a green-house or conservatory, if only because it's the only orchid species that is of commercial significance.

## Zygopetalum

**Origins:** Brazil
*Zygopetalum* species have been cultivated for a long time, but many hybrids have recently come onto the market.

Trichopilia tortilis *with its corkscrew-shaped sepals makes an excellent houseplant.*

**Treatment:** *Zygopetalum* is a typical conservatory plant, with a captivating scent and flowers that last for several weeks. It needs a lot of light in order to flower. If plants are well cared for, the leaves will be light rather than dark green in colour. Summer temperatures should be 21–23°C (70–73°F) during the daytime and 13–14°C (55–57°F) at night; winter temperatures should be lower. Always keep the plant slightly moist and use plenty of fertiliser. Scarcely any rest period is required.

# Useful addresses

**Royal Horticultural Society**
80 Vincent Square, London SW1P 2PE
tel. 020 7834 4333
e-mail: info@rhs.org.uk
website: http://www.rhs.org.uk

Advice and information on buying and growing orchids. Publishers of the world's longest-standing orchid periodical, *The Orchid Review*, with up-to-date lists of new orchid hybrids.

**Sander's List of Orchid Hybrids**
International Orchid Register
2 Albert Street, Stapleford, Nottingham NG9 8DB
tel. 0115 939 2828
Available on CD-ROM as *RHS Orchids 98*

**The Orchid Society of Great Britain**
website: http://www.orchid-society-gb.com
Membership Secretary, 39 Hainault Road,
Romford, Essex RM5 3AA

Publishes its own journal and provides information about local orchid societies throughout the UK.

**Scottish Orchid Society**
c/o 164 Eskhill, Penicuik, Midlothian EH26 8DQ
tel. 01968 677075

**Orchid Suppliers**

**Burnham Nurseries Ltd**
Forches Cross, Newton Abbot, Devon TQ12 6PZ
tel. 01626 352233

**McBean's Orchids**
Cooksbridge, Lewes, East Sussex BN8 4PR
tel. 01273 400228

**Deva Orchids**
Littlebrook Farm, Stryt Isa, Pen-y-Fordd, Chester CH4 0JY
tel. 01978 762454

**Equatorial Plant Company**
7 Grey Lane, Barnard Castle, Durham DL12 8PD
tel. 01833 690519

**Ivens Orchids**
'Great Barn Dell', St Albans Road, Sandridge,
St Albans, Herts AL4 9LB
tel. 01727 863178

**David Stead Orchids**
Greenscapes Horticultural Centre, Brandon
Crescent, Shadwell, Leeds LS17 6JH
tel. 0113 289 3933

# Index